LIVING
BRAVE

SHANNON DINGLE

HarperOne
An Imprint of HarperCollins*Publishers*

LIVING
BRAVE

LESSONS

FROM HURT,

LIGHTING

THE WAY

TO HOPE

LIVING BRAVE. Copyright © 2021 by Shannon Dingle. All rights reserved. Printed in the United States of America. No part of this book may be used or reproduced in any manner whatsoever without written permission except in the case of brief quotations embodied in critical articles and reviews. For information, address HarperCollins Publishers, 195 Broadway, New York, NY 10007.

HarperCollins books may be purchased for educational, business, or sales promotional use. For information, please email the Special Markets Department at SPsales@harpercollins.com.

FIRST HARPERCOLLINS PAPERBACK PUBLISHED IN 2022

Library of Congress Cataloging-in-Publication Data is available upon request.

ISBN 978-0-06-295928-7

22 23 24 25 26   LSC   10 9 8 7 6 5 4 3 2 1

FOR LEE,
MY PARTNER
MY WORLD
MY SAFE
MY HOME
MY ECSTASY
MY COMFORT
EVERY GOOD THING
THANK YOU FOR TEACHING ME MY BELOVEDNESS

CONTENTS

CONTENTS

LIVING
BRAVE

YOU HAVE PERMISSION (AND SO DO I)

This is not the book I planned to write.

I planned to write as a woman who had survived unimaginable trauma but lived into a mostly happily-ever-after. I planned to write from scars rather than wounds. I planned to walk with you down a path I had already traversed.

I planned for my husband to be alive.

I never planned for a week at the beach to end with organ donation paperwork. I never planned for Lee to be out with most of our kids, playing in the sand and water, as he had so many times before, when a wave hit him hard enough to slam his head to the ground, immediately breaking his neck, severing nerves controlling the lungs and heart, and causing enough swelling to cut off his airway. I never planned to go from the beach, shins still covered in sand from kneeling beside him as paramedics worked to do all they could, to the hospital and then back to the beach house as a widow rather than a wife. I never planned to have to tell my six children that Daddy was dead. I never planned to answer all the hard questions that would come in the following days and weeks and months (and years, I'm sure, though we aren't there yet). I never planned to say goodbye when we were both only thirty-seven years old.

I never planned to live so many stories I've written in these pages.

He wasn't even supposed to die before me. My health is complicated; his wasn't. When we talked about the future, we both assumed I would die first. I was going to leave him, not the other way around.

But not in our thirties. Not when we had so much more left to do together. Not without seeing our kids grow up and become who God created them to be. Not right after a major promotion for him and a book deal for me, the first of many, I hope. Not with plans to visit Ireland again and to start a new stage of life together when our youngest turned eighteen the year we would turn forty-eight. We were going to do so many things.

As for me, I was going to write this book from the safety and stability of our relationship.

I can't write that book anymore. That book died in the ICU in Wilmington, North Carolina, when Lee did. Parts of it will survive the edits and rewrites, just as parts of his body live on: his heart in the chest of a man in his forties, his liver in a lawyer and husband in his seventies, and one of his kidneys in the body of a mom of five in her forties who loves cooking and yoga, a woman with whom I'd probably be friends if we met in a casual setting. (Well, maybe. I like eating and wearing yoga pants, so that's nearly the same, right?)

The first draft of my manuscript was almost done, and then it wasn't. It was rich and true and beautiful. But this grief I carry changes everything, so I found myself reworking almost everything. With such a catastrophic loss, there's a before and after.

My before draft didn't match my after reality.

This is not the book I planned to write, but I'm giving myself permission to write the book I need to write. I'm giving myself permission to show up with my words to you, my dear reader, and to tell the truth, even the messiest and most shattered pieces of it. I'm giving us all permission to come to these pages with all of ourselves because every bit of who I am and who you are matters.

———

Life forces bravery on us all at different times. Something catastrophic happens, and any way of continuing in the after is a brave path.

Maybe it's a diagnosis. A breakup. An epically or ordinarily bad day. A death, maybe of a person, maybe of a dream, maybe of the life you always imagined but would never get to live. A kid waking up in the middle of the night covered in vomit, and you have to be the grown-up. A moment in which you feel like you're chickening out because you're saying no to something and you've forgotten that no can be the bravest word when a yes is expected. A natural disaster leaving you with pieces from before to bring into this after existence. A global pandemic in which the best after scenario will still be cataclysmically different from any before.

Maybe it's actually something amazing and good and saturated with joy, but the newness of it all means that moving forward is terrifying, which means that each step must be brave. Moving somewhere new. Coming out. A child entering your life. A child moving away for their next stage in life. Something you created going viral. Someone who loves you growing closer. A windfall. A new job. Leaving a job you hate.

The world is made of stories, and yours is part of that. Your brave is being real in a world that shouts, "Be yourself," followed by, "No, not like that!" Your brave will bring mistakes because brave spaces aren't meant to be safe spaces or comfort zones or perfection prisons. Embracing the brave that is yours will mean you might let others down, but you'll learn that's better than letting yourself down over and over.

To be clear, bravery is never meant to be an excuse to be a dick. Some people will use it that way, but that's not really brave, y'all. That's a jackass in a unicorn costume, one that looks something like bravery but is just hiding what's underneath. The costume doesn't change the core, and eventually the jackass makes itself known.

Reader, you are not the jackass.

Most of us have been told who we are is bad or wrong or less than others, maybe by parents, maybe by faith communities, maybe by rarely or never seeing someone who looks like you as a main character or on a magazine cover or in the White House or in the classroom. Living brave requires us to know ourselves and give ourselves permission to be that person, not the version others have handed to us like a unicorn costume. Unicorns are awesome—don't get me wrong—but you being you is more majestic.

I'm a Christian, and I frame living brave for myself through the lens of my faith as "becoming all of who God made me to be." I know that might sound triggering to those of you who have experienced religious trauma. For me, though, it works because I'm clear in my mind that God's self-proclaimed representatives are not God.

When we're brave, we'll make some people unhappy. But we aren't meant to become all of the person [fill in the blank here] thinks we should be. You have permission to deviate from that path, but that's not an offering from me. It's already yours; it was given by your Creator and cannot be repossessed by anyone else.

You are you. I am me. And that's how it's supposed to be.

As an example, I know you might be mildly annoyed by the title of this book because, yes, it is grammatically incorrect. Per the rules of the English language, "living bravely" is what's proper. I'll explain the reason for the title, even though I've learned that being brave can be as simple as deciding other people aren't owed an explanation for every decision. It can be brave to answer, "I'm me, and this was my choice," without anything more detailed than that.

When my (now dead) husband, Lee, was in elementary school, he always thought he was in trouble. "Walk quietly," the teacher would stage-whisper to the class. "Come along quickly," if they were too slow. "Listen carefully," if they weren't. None of those exhortations were uncommon in school settings, but Lee heard them differently than the rest of us did. He heard, "Walk quiet, Lee," and "Come along quick, Lee," and "Listen careful, Lee!" Every phrase sounded like he was being singled out from everyone else.

So many of my present-day brave stories come back to Lee. I was living bravely before I met him, of course. He didn't make me brave.

But now? I'm living bravely without Lee, which is another level of impossible.

I'm living brave. No "-ly," because no Lee.

———

What do you need to give yourself permission to be or do? (You don't have to linger here long, just start your brain engine on that question for now.)

As I wrote in the beginning, I'm giving myself permission for this book to be completely different than I had planned, having written most of it before I became a widow and single mom of six at age thirty-seven. I had plenty of content already, but now everything is tinted with the death of my husband who won't turn thirty-eight or thirty-nine or eighty-nine along with me.

Remember when memories turned a bit blue in the film *Inside Out* when Sadness touched them? That's real. Every part of who I am and how I live brave is colored by saying goodbye to Lee and then telling our children the horrible news and then learning how to exist without him.

But hear me loud and clear on this: comparative suffering has no place in living brave. Just because my personal permission slip is weighty enough to have become an international news story doesn't mean your permission slip means any less. No, your struggles are real. So are mine. That's all we have to honor, rather than trying to medal in any sort of Oppression Olympics. The hardest thing each of us is facing doesn't have to be put on a scale to decide who has it worse. No, we survive and thrive together in our common humanity. Together, we collectively bear the weight of what it means—the horrible and the wonderful—to be human.

———

I threw away a children's book last week. It was a book about bravery, where the lesson was that being brave means saying or doing the hard thing.

I threw it away because I didn't want my kids to learn the lie that bravery is always saying yes and never no. Bravery isn't always flashy. Sometimes bravery is walking away. I want my children—and you, my reader—to know courage comes in many forms.

This book will be about giving ourselves permission to be brave without following any cultural script for what brave looks like on a big screen or in headlines. Sure, brave can be lauded and public, but brave can also be the quiet act of doing the next best thing.

In the first part of the book, we'll explore survival as brave, granting ourselves permission to take hard steps (chapter 1) and face necessary grief (chapter 2).

Next, I challenge us to reject the idea that speaking out is always the brave choice. Instead, choosing your voice—including when to use it and when not to—is brave, with powerful words (chapter 3), not keeping secrets (chapter 4), and hard truths (chapter 5).

In a culture in which being a lone hero is presented as brave, it's countercultural to give ourselves permission to trust, even though that might be the bravest choice of all. Living brave, after all, requires us to decide what we believe (chapter 6) and evaluate how, when, and if we trust others (chapter 7).

Yet we can't be truly brave unless we are bold enough to take care of ourselves, recognizing that our desires are important (chapter 8), our feelings are good information (chapter 9), and health matters (chapter 10).

The next part of living brave is the hardest for me. As a survivor of abuse and a grieving widow who lost my most precious relationship with the speed of a wave, being in relationship with others feels too vulnerable. That's precisely what makes it brave, as we endure hard conversations (chapter 11) and choose our own family (chapter 12).

Finally, hope is brave. The conclusion consists of one chapter about whether hope still exists (chapter 13), with a handful of essays that explain why my answer is still yes: because we don't know it all, because none of us is broken, because we all belong, and because the light still shines.

None of this will look the same for everyone. This isn't a self-help book full of prescriptive how-tos. I'm a fan of those books, but living brave isn't about rules or fitting in. Living brave is about research, both the published-in-journals kind and the survived-in-struggles kind. I'm bringing all I have to this book: my grad school research in inclusive education, my childhood secrets of abuse and sex trafficking, my lifelong obsession with trauma studies, my identity as a disabled woman, my lessons learned as a mom of six kids from three continents by birth and adoption, my late-night literature reviews of medical data available for any of my or their chronic conditions, my shock and grief when our beach vacation turned to tragedy, my intensive-enough-that-I-should-have-earned-a-degree-by-now hours in therapy, and my body's and psyche's personification of the word "rare" even when all I wanted was sameness.

Is this a memoir? Is this a work of creative nonfiction? Is this based in social sciences or life experience? The answers are yes, yes, yes, and yes. But more than anything, this book is an invitation. There's a blank page in front of all of us. We can live into it, imperfectly and bravely and with inevitable failures but also terrifying joys, or we can keep staring at it, passing over the pen so someone else can write our story for us.

I'm the first kind of person, and I think maybe you are too. Only you can decide that. Living brave is no light task, and some of the stories I'll tell are hard to read, so before the first chapter, I want you to pause for a moment:

Breathe in for four counts,
hold that breath for four counts,
breathe out for four counts, and
hold again for four.

This is called box breathing, and when I do it, I draw a box with my finger in the air: up as I breathe in, to the right as I hold it, down for the exhale, and to the left as I hold that. Then I begin again.

For my kids, we have boxes made with blue painter's tape on the walls throughout our house to give a visual cue and tactile process for their own box breathing.

I'm teaching you this as a way of equipping you not only for life but also for reading this book, because I'll be sharing sometimes about being forced to live brave in the most disturbing of circumstances. In hindsight, this is a strategy that might have been handy on the first page or two as I shared the story of saying goodbye to the life I thought I'd be living and the book I thought I'd be writing.

Let's do one more box: inhale up, 2, 3, 4, hold to the right, 2, 3, 4, exhale down, 2, 3, 4, hold to the left, 2, 3, 4.

Now that you've steadied yourself with this simple but effective strategy, it's permission slip time. What do you give yourself permission to do or be or think or anything as you join me in living brave? Write or draw it, or tell a friend, or choreograph an interpretive dance about it if you'd like.

Once you're done with that, let's go,
with permission to be eager or afraid,
tentative or reckless,
skimming these words or fully committing to them,
writing expected stories or ones we never could have imagined,
and anything in between.

There is no such thing as a "safe space"—
We exist in the real world.
We all carry scars and have caused wounds.
This space
seeks to turn down the volume of the world outside,
and amplify voices that have to fight to be heard
elsewhere,
This space will not be perfect.
It will not always be what we wish it to be
But
It will be our space together,
and we will work on it side by side.

BY BETH SPRANO

PART I

SURVIVING IS BRAVE

CHAPTER 1

HARD STEPS

healing only begins
when
hurt is acknowledged

As I write this chapter, it's fall of 2019, with my youngest child's birthday coming this week and Halloween the next. My partner in all things died three months ago today. I miss everything about him: his smell, which never quite came out of T-shirts in the wash, the reassuring heat of his breath on my neck as I drifted to sleep, the rhythm of his heart when I laid my head on his chest, the safety of his arms wrapped around me. I wish I didn't remember his unnatural facial movements or pale skin or barely there pulse as I knelt by his side on the beach while the paramedics tried to save him. I hate that a simple vacation day at the beach turned fatal.

I didn't know how I would tell my kids Daddy wasn't coming home. I didn't know how to love them well through this nightmare, especially the kids we'd adopted who had already experienced the death of a parent. I didn't know how to live as an adult, much less a single mom of six, without my best friend. I didn't know how we would survive without his paycheck, how our extensive medical needs would be covered without his employer-based insurance, how my arthritic hands would open too-tight bottles and jars, how to pay the bills, or even what bills we had.

I did know that my inclination in times of stress is to isolate, to curl myself into a cocoon and not see light or life until I am ready to emerge again. I also knew that tendency wouldn't lead to healing. That trauma response involves telling myself it will protect me, yet it separates me from human connection, from not only loss but also love. I needed every bit of myself, every bit of God, and every bit of our community to do any of the hard steps that would come.

My boss at the nonprofit I left in 2016 was a staunch believer in five-year plans. I hated them then. I hate them more now. If I were wearing a headlamp, my plans for now would only be the things in the light. Anything else can wait until I get there.

Doing all the paperwork so his organs could be donated was easy. Nothing else was.

I had to decide early on if I wanted cremation or burial, and the world flipped upside down. This was not what I should be deciding for my thirty-seven-year-old husband. My therapist wisely asked me about Ugandan traditions because three of our children were adopted at older ages from there, and that made the decision: cremation was taboo in their village, so burial it was. The other choices that week were harder—a casket, a vault for the casket, a gravesite, the clothes in which he would be buried, the details for the funeral—and I thought decisions would get easier in time.

They haven't.

In Donald Hall's exquisite poem "Distressed Haiku,"[1] I found these truth-carrying words:

You think that their
dying is the worst
thing that could happen.

Then they stay dead.

Living while Lee stays dead is the worst and bravest thing, because now the past is bittersweet, the present is empty of him, and the future we planned was hard steps we'll never take together.

My favorite president is known for many things: loving the Constitution, concealing a medical condition from the public, sacrificially stepping down during his daughter's kidnapping, and saying, "What's next?"

Yes, he's fictional, but I don't care. I think the world would be a better place today if President Bartlet from *The West Wing* was in the Oval. I'm not sure how, but I didn't notice his habit of saying, "What's next?" until my fourth or fifth time binge-watching the series. (Confession: I've lost count of the number of times I've rewatched every episode. I'm not even a little embarrassed by that. I'm a little embarrassed for you if you haven't seen it yet, so put down this book and turn on Netflix, okay? I'll be here waiting for you when you're done.)

His "What's next?" signaled a transition: what happened beforehand mattered, but now it's time to turn toward the next task, the next ask, the next action. Maybe I didn't notice the common phrase at first because it's how I often approach life, especially when all is well. I'm trying to learn to slow down and savor the victories, instead of immediately shifting to whatever challenge is ahead.

When I fail, though, I'm all about the postmortem. I mostly hate sports, but I am a pro at Monday morning quarterbacking. I excel in analyzing how the pieces could have fallen differently if only I did something different. If something went wrong, I generally blame me. For every person I love (and some people I've never even met), I'm a fabulous defense attorney. I have your back. I'm fiercely loyal. For me, though? I transform into the most vicious prosecutor.

Some of my closest friends know this about me. They know when it's time to suggest a "What's next?" sort of pivot. None, however, have ever been as precious or needed as Brenda's "What's next?" in March of 2004.

I was twenty-one and well into my first year of teaching middle school. Having graduated college at age twenty, I didn't dare let any of my students know how young I really was. I had started drinking early in middle school and drank on and off—mostly on—since then. In my final year of college, I cut back. I saw risk factors for the alcoholism that ran deep in my family.

Immediately after graduation, I moved to Texas to start a new position, teaching middle school special education in Rio Grande City as part of Teach for America. When I turned twenty-one on our first day of training, I thought my drinking problems were over. I attributed all of my previous alcohol issues to being too young and breaking the law. Now I could drink legally, so I was sure that meant I would also magically be able to drink wisely.

That didn't go so well.

Growing up as the youngest child in a house of alcoholics, I had a front-row seat to a lot of inebriated foolishness. I prayed through multiple drives with a drunk parent behind the wheel. My sister and I once convinced our older brother not to sleep in the driveway because birds might poop in his mouth. I couldn't count the number of times I helped my mom stumble back to her bed or grabbed a blanket to tuck in my dad where he had passed out in his recliner. I swore I would never be like them. I drank, yes, but I was always going to drink smart. I set firm rules for myself to avoid ever being a burden on anyone else like they had been on me at times.

I had learned well in my childhood home to be a functional substance abuser, so I never missed school. As a teacher, I excelled enough to be featured in a teaching textbook for new teachers. I sang with the church worship team and served with the local chapter of the Jaycees and mentored a group of middle school girls once a week after the bell rang. I also danced on bars and took a lot of tequila shots and probably smelled like alcohol at times when I thought I didn't. I lived and taught in a small town where the closest movie theater was in Mexico and the fanciest restaurant in town was the brand-new Denny's. My weekend routine consisted of sitting with my roommate, Niki, on the patio of our house on the Rio Grande River, drinking whatever booze we had, and watching the Border Patrol drive back and forth. Life was good, or so I thought.

But then, the year I turned twenty-one, I started breaking all the rules. I started drinking stuff I didn't even like because I wanted to be numb to the feelings starting to surface now that I was fully independent of my family. I drank alone more and more. I tried to restrict myself to one drink, but one always turned into six. By the time I broke my biggest rule—the vow to never drive drunk—I didn't even know who I was anymore.

I kept on living my public life as if I were a teetotaler. No one at my Southern Baptist church knew that I drank, not even Brenda, my closest friend and coleader for youth group. I wrote my lesson plans and implemented them well. I showed up to service projects whenever I said I would. I basically lived two separate lives.

Those lives collided at a writing teachers' conference in Austin. Our school sent a group of us on Thursday for the training, and then a handful of our fellow teachers from other disciplines drove up to join us once school let out for the weekend. Friday night, we headed to Sixth Street. Because I had never had a good fake ID and didn't turn twenty-one until after I graduated from college, this was my first time barhopping in any significant way. I felt so grown up, which is almost always a good sign that you aren't. By the time our science and history teacher friends found us, we were at our fourth or fifth bar. I'm not sure I can trust that recollection, though, because math can get hard for me after a few drinks. The number of drinks I had consumed was still-able-to-walk-but-having-trouble-not-falling-off-my-barstool. Even though I was already engaged to the man who would become my husband, I used my old college trick of letting the bartender eat from a candy necklace worn around my neck in exchange for free drinks. No, that act wasn't dignified, but I craved alcohol like oxygen and lived on a teacher's salary. I told myself nothing was wrong with what I was doing.

After I got my last drink, I sat at a pub table and closed my eyes until the room stopped feeling like a rocking ship at sea. When I opened my eyes, my friend Scott was across from me.

Well, "friend" might be too strong of a word. We arrived in South Texas through the same program, taught at the same school, and circulated in similar friend groups. I always got a weird vibe from him, though. Since I suck at small talk when I'm sober and lose all ability to engage in it when I'm not, I blurted out, "I don't think you like me very much. Why is that? Did I do something wrong?"

He looked surprised. He paused to gather his thoughts, which he could do because he was a few bars and several drinks behind me. Meanwhile, I focused my energy on pretending to be more sober than I was and trying not to fall off my barstool. (I still wonder why bars have stools instead of chairs that keep your feet safely grounded once you're snockered.)

"I do like you," he started. My face must have broadcast my skepticism, because he backtracked. "I can see why you think I don't. I'm confused by you." He inhaled deeply. I waited. He began again. "I've never known a Christian who was intelligent, who thought through her faith instead of just feeling it and following others. I don't know what to do with that. I don't know what to do with you."

He took a shot, maybe vodka. I pulled at my candy necklace and chewed the edges, while swirling my finger in the condensation on the outside of my glass. Mostly, I didn't want to make eye contact. Someone called his name, and he touched my hand for a second and then turned away.

I stared into my drink, looking for answers to the disarray Scott's words had called forth in me. As usual, I never found the solution I sought in the bottom of a glass. As usual, liquor was helping me erase questions for a night so I didn't have to ponder anything. But this time, the question began to unravel me before I had sobered up or even stood up.

I didn't finish the drink in front of me. I wanted to be everything Scott had described, but I knew I couldn't keep living divided within myself. I knew my inauthenticity didn't reflect the God I loved; it didn't serve anyone's good, not even my own. I wanted to cry, even though I had never been that drunk girl crying at a party. I blinked back tears, knowing I needed to change something but not knowing if I could.

———

The rest of the night was a fog, and not just from my blood alcohol level shooting through the roof. I was still a little drunk the next morning, wearing sunglasses as I ate my toast. We drove home later that day, and I pretended my silence was from the hangover. My pretending skills were well honed from childhood, so no one guessed anything different. I didn't know yet that I was done drinking for more than a decade. I didn't even believe then that a girl like me, drinking regularly since age eleven and occasionally well before that, could ever be done drinking. I just knew something inside me felt awry, but I hadn't noticed until then.

I made myself busy as soon as I got home. My roommate had quit our teaching program a few months earlier and had moved back to Maryland, so it was just me and the two cats I kept in our breakup as roomies. I've always been a bit of a slob, but I needed a distraction, so I started cleaning. By that evening, the house was cleaner than it had ever been since I moved in. I planned to rest once my favorite show, *Alias*, came on. Jennifer Garner's badassery was a cure for all things.

Brenda loved *Alias* too. Rolando, her husband, was working in the ER that night, so every time a commercial break started, she called me or I called her so we could analyze what had just happened between Sydney and Vaughn and Spy Daddy (aka Jack). This was serious business. We didn't joke around when it came to the Bristows.

The show ended, she called me, and we wrapped up our analysis. Then I got quiet. Every friend knows that a quiet Shannon is a troubled Shannon. Thankfully, Brenda waited, saying nothing and trusting that I would speak once I was ready.

"I got really drunk this weekend," I blurted out.

Before that moment, Brenda didn't know I drank. She was part of my dry life, which I had compartmentalized from my alcohol-rich one. She had no preparation for my words. I winced after I realized what I had just said, bracing for judgment or at least shock. It didn't come.

Instead, in a steady tone, she simply asked, "So what are you going to do now?"

Her question changed me. Her question asked me to look forward. Her question accepted my past for what it was and used my present to spark my imagination for what could be. She invited me to dream of a different sort of life. It was the first of three "What's next?" questions that would set me on a different course after that week.

A few days later, over dinner at Denny's, I poured out my jumbled thoughts on my friend Dave, talking mostly about how I didn't think I should drink anymore. He listened. As I finished and dug into my French toast, he asked another pivotal question for me: "Do you think you're an alcoholic? That sounds like what you're describing."

I hadn't seen that for myself yet. I had resolved that I would never be like my parents in that way, and as a high achiever, I usually succeeded at my goals. Substance use disorders don't respect work ethic, though. As I heard his careful words, I wasn't positive "alcoholic" was a label that fit me well, but I knew that he was offering a crucial piece to my life puzzle. I also knew I would need to be sober, maybe for a while and maybe forever, to heal.

The third life-changing question that week came from my coworker Annabel. She was the school's guidance counselor for the kids I taught. As I sat in her office at lunch, I worked up the courage to tell her what was going on. She said she was proud of me. Then she challenged me with the question that completed my life's turnabout, resetting the path my childhood had taught me to follow.

"What's the real issue, though? Substance abuse and other addiction is about hiding from something else. What are you hiding from?"

I've never felt so vulnerably exposed and so lovingly known as I did in that moment. She saw me. She knew my pain wasn't about alcohol. She encouraged me to go to therapy for the first time and do the hard healing work that got me sober and healthy enough to marry Lee a year and a half later.

Without Brenda and Dave and Annabel helping me seek sobriety and wholeness through their different "What's next?" challenges, I don't think I'd be alive today. Avoidance via alcohol was killing me. They lent me the bravery to explore what life could be without it, when I wasn't sure I could survive sober. As it was, I was barely making it drunk. They taught me that I didn't have to merely survive when I could truly live.

"What's next?" can be a terrifying question to answer, especially when it feels like we're operating without a net. Self-destruction felt safer to me at first. But all the rewards of life—deep feelings, belly laughs, tears of joy and empathy, hugs that feel like clouds—are out there. I learned that I can do this, whatever the next thing is.

(I wrote those last words before the film *Frozen II* came out. If you haven't listened to it yet, stop right now and find Kristen Bell's emotive ballad "The Next Right Thing" on the soundtrack. I mean it. Listen. Now.)

———

Nowadays I can recite Donald Hall's haiku from memory. The choices aren't getting easier because Lee stays dead. They're different, but I think life from now on will be nothing but hard steps made harder by his absence.

For church, the hard step is showing up without him. I'm taking that step on the Sundays I can, but I'm not ready for the step of singing a single line about God's goodness. I'm not ready for singing most other lines either. I'm not ready for opening my Bible. I'm not even open to paying attention some mornings, opting for games on my phone as I sit alone in the pew, preferring it that way because it feels lonely without him but the presence of anyone else can feel intrusive. Faith for me looks like showing up and letting others hold belief for me when my hands are too full of pain for anything else to fit.

My tragedy is too recent to know what any long-term anything might look like. I'm okay with that. The hardest steps are the ones I can only see one at a time, when I can't predict the next one or the one after that. Those are the only steps there ever are, though, I'm realizing. None of us knows when a wave might literally or figuratively wash away every step we expect to take in the future. I'm not being Morbid Morticia or Debby Downer; I'm simply telling the truth. We like control, predictability, plans. We like to think that if we do x, then y will happen. We want to pretend vulnerability isn't at the core of being human, but it is.

Give yourself permission to take one step at a time while holding anticipated steps loosely. We don't know what's next. That's why taking steps one at a time is so damn hard. It always feels like a tightrope without any net.

And it is.

Living brave requires us to take the next step anyway. It's worth it, dammit, but it also totally sucks at times. Let it suck, and do the next thing.

Both/and.

CHAPTER 2

NECESSARY GRIEF

I love the Thursday Jesus
who prays to our Abba
to offer another way to salvation
other than the painful road ahead
I love the Saturday people
who live in the tension
of already promises but
not yet realities
still believing in this Messiah
but questioning in the dark
if he can really do what he said
We celebrate Sunday
as Easter
and
commemorate Friday
as Good
but I love me some
Thursday Jesus
and
Saturday people

t was an ordinary day at the beach, until it wasn't.

I sat crisscross on our bed, my laptop open, writing an earlier version of this book. I could see the sand and waves and kites and people from the second floor of the beach house we rented for the week, but my eyes were fixed on the screen as words formed into the story I thought you'd be holding in your hands right now.

As I said in the beginning, this book, the one you are holding, is not the one I meant to write.

This story is not the one I meant to live.

The practice of living brave is unchanged, but the agony for me is now a wound rather than a scar. We all like tidy stories, where stitches are long gone and a shiny line in the skin, preferably faint, is all that's left. I have more than twenty surgical scars on my body, some healed neatly and some whose color, size, or texture makes them more prominent, but any one of them is prettier than something unhealed.

Or maybe that's a lie to unlearn. Maybe the most beautiful scene is that of a bloody and bruised heart still beating. Maybe the miracle isn't in the healing but in the living, even through hell.

On my right upper arm, I have a piece of art tattooed, which was originally drawn by my friend Melissa. It's an anatomical heart, with bandages and stitches and, added after Lee's death, drops of blood. But from the heart, flowers bloom, some original to the tattoo itself and some added after Lee died as a personal declaration that I would see life grow from pain yet again. I'm still waiting for that.

My husband's donated heart still beats, albeit in the chest of a man I'm not ready to meet. My heart felt like it stopped that day and now carries on a new rhythm in a different person because I am no longer and will never be the same person I was on the morning of July 18, 2019, the person who didn't know how cruel that evening would be.

I like the person I'm becoming, but I miss the old me. She didn't know the truth of this excerpt from "Blessing for the Brokenhearted"[2] by Jan Richardson, that

Perhaps for now
it can be enough
to simply marvel
at the mystery
of how a heart
so broken
can go on beating

Sometimes I wish none of us ever had to learn that mystery at all.

———

The beach day made me into a grief expert overnight. That's a role no one wants because, to gain expertise, you have to first endure gutting loss. My husband died in the freakiest of freak accidents, and my tragedy played out in stories every hour on news stations around the world.

People witnessed me write through the process with naked words, starting with the ones I drafted in the hours after we knew Lee was dead but before a formal declaration could be made. North Carolina doesn't allow brain death to be called until electrolytes are balanced. As they started the IV drip, I turned to my friend Lindsey and sighed. "Gatorade is not going to fix this." Not knowing what else to do, I opened an empty memo in my phone, and began writing:

My partner, my love, and my home died today after a freak accident. Lee was playing on the beach with three of our kids yesterday, and an intense wave hit him just right to slam his head into the sand, break his neck, and make his throat swell so much his brain was deprived of oxygen for too long to recover. Some heroes—including our kids—tried to save him, but it wouldn't have mattered what they did. His body couldn't recover from the initial injury.

We met when I was 18 and he was 19, and we've been together ever since. I wasn't supposed to be saying goodbye at 37. I don't know how to be a grown-up without him, but I'll learn. I just wish I didn't have to.

Details to come about all the things. Please pray for us. And, you know, feel free to cuss and smash stuff because God knows I'll be doing some of that. (And breathing and hydrating and eating and all those self-care things because I am worth it and because I have six little people to parent.)

My words were so deliberate that some questioned whether I was scamming people for sympathy and donations. But words have been grounding for me, so when I knew my husband was dying, I sat in an empty procedure room to write what I would later share and create an album of images on my phone to post with those words.

As I've processed and continue to process what it means to be a widow, I don't know how to offer anything but raw, honest, and naked words. I didn't realize this was rare at first, until the comments and messages started, as readers thanked me for the permission my grief gave them to grieve too. They didn't use these exact words, but they bore sacred witness as I was grieving brave, living brave, through searing loss, and they received that as a gift somehow.

Watching me become a grief scholar in real time, people began asking questions. Most of them were versions of this: how do we live in an uncertain world, knowing grief can knock on the door at any moment? We just do. No guidelines exist, and that's precisely why showing up to life every day is brave. We do the next thing, often without knowing the next one after that. We give ourselves permission to do nothing at all sometimes. We look head-on at whatever we're facing. We cry. We laugh. We grieve. We rejoice.

We live brave in a world that offers no guarantees, except

that it will change and some of those changes will leave lasting bruises on our souls.

The words of Ecclesiastes 3:1–8 (NRSV) come to mind:

For everything there is a season, and a time for every matter under
    heaven:

a time to be born, and a time to die;
a time to plant, and a time to pluck up what is planted;
a time to kill, and a time to heal;
a time to break down, and a time to build up;
a time to weep, and a time to laugh;
a time to mourn, and a time to dance;
a time to throw away stones, and a time to gather stones together;
a time to embrace, and a time to refrain from embracing;
a time to seek, and a time to lose;
a time to keep, and a time to throw away;
a time to tear, and a time to sew;
a time to keep silence, and a time to speak;
a time to love, and a time to hate;
a time for war, and a time for peace.

As I did some research into those verses, I came across them used in two places. The first, as I expected, were in writings based on the Hebrew Bible. The other was poetry websites and anthologies.

I was surprised by that, but it makes sense. These words hold universal truth in the rhythms of rich language. They capture the uncertainty in which we live. We don't care for some of those times—the dying and the weeping and the mourning and the killing of things inside us that need to die and the losing and the tearing and the silence and the hate and the war—but we cherish others: the healing and the laughing and the dancing and the embracing and the love and the peace. But as one of my favorite researcher/storytellers, Brené Brown, has learned and shared, we can't numb the darkness without also numbing the light. In one of her popular TED talks,[3] she said, "You cannot selectively numb emotion. When we numb [hard feelings], we numb joy, we numb gratitude, we numb happiness." Life exists in the balance, in the pendulum's swing, and in uncertainty more than certainty most of the time.

During my first years of rheumatoid arthritis, after being diagnosed at twenty-four, I grieved the life I expected to have, the life that had been replaced by constant pain and a cane in my twenties. An earnest couple in our Sunday school class asked if they could pray for me. I liked them, and I believe in the magic of prayer, so I said yes. We sat down. They laid their hands on my hands, a sweet gesture. But then they prayed, and I wish I hadn't been too stunned to speak or walk out.

"God, we know you can heal Shannon if she has enough faith."

Nope. The couple was well-meaning, but blaming someone's illness on a lack of faith isn't okay. It's in those moments that I wish the Nickelodeon slime were real and could be dropped whenever someone does something particularly egregious. (Fun fact: Because of liability concerns, that slime had to be edible. It was mostly vanilla pudding and food coloring.) No, my body was in a season of breaking down, and nothing in their blame game helped build me up. Grief is scary, but it's less scary than arrogantly misplaced religious certainty.

We don't need to do Christianity or faith or life better. We do whatever the next right thing is, be that resting or working or napping or playing or zoning out for a bit on social media or with Netflix. More than anything, through chronic illnesses and life in general, I've learned that grief doesn't give a damn if you like it or not. It's there anyway. It's a part of life. So I notice it, give a slight nod its way, and then go on doing my own thing.

And sometimes, even if you do all the right things, a healthy man can end up dead with a broken neck from a rogue wave. That's a fun reminder my life offers.

———

"Fuck."

That's the single word I texted in July 2015 in response to my childhood friend, Lisa. Her text was letting me know that her four-year-old son, Eli, had died during the night. I read the text in the morning. I'm not one to recklessly use profanity (or I wasn't back then), but polite words fail when a little boy dies. (She replied with the same word when Lee died on the same date four years later.)

Throughout Eli's illness and bone marrow transplant, people far and wide followed his story online. Then and later, after his death, someone would drop a platitude of certainty, from the true but twisted and poorly timed "God works all things for the good" to the false "God will never give you more than you can handle." As they offered pithy attempts at empathy, it seemed none of them had ever come across Proverbs 25:20 (NIV): "Like one who takes away a garment on a cold day, or like vinegar poured on a wound, is one who sings songs to a heavy heart." I take that as God's way of telling us to hold space for the suffering rather than rushing it along.

The worst of the statements, though, wasn't true though it was earnest: "I can't imagine."

We look away from pain because we want to skip the mess. We like the time before the mess, and we like to talk about the mess after it's cleaned up. But the mess itself? We hate that. We avoid that. We even deny that. We run from our own messes with substance abuse, sex, eating disorders, busyness, Netflix binges, porn, and a variety of other vices or good things taken to a vice-level extreme. We turn our back on other people's messes with avoidance, ghosting, unavailability, and, yes, offering clichés that only serve to make the speaker feel better but not the listener.

Suffering that can't be fixed can only be carried. We need each other. Some pain is too big to be carried alone. One way we survive in an uncertain world is by togetherness, even in the mess. We belong to each other. When uncertainty feels unbearable, we let others in to help us bear the messiness. In another season, we might be shored up enough to lean into someone else's mess right when they need it. We're not meant to be bystanders. No, we're firefighters who run into the burning building, just not in the literal sense. We run into the mess, even if we see no way out. Sometimes sitting with someone in the dark uncertainty is all we need to do.

————

Of course, more mundane reminders of uncertainty show up all the time. Just last week, one of my younger daughters did a cartwheel and managed to plant one of her hands squarely on a bee in the process. The bee did what bees do in response to danger and stung her. The fun afternoon I expected of kids playing in the backyard while I worked on my latest article for *Teen Vogue* was over. My writing got set aside, as the uncertainty that comes with parenthood shattered my original plans. Instead, I snuggled and read books with my girl, while monitoring her breathing because she has some allergies but had never been stung before so we didn't know how her little acrobatic body would respond. Nothing happened, thankfully. Meanwhile, I got nothing done while simultaneously attending to everything important.

I've been thinking a lot lately about when that precious daughter and her two biological siblings joined our family. It's been six years as I write this. Lee and I flew to Uganda with an almost-two-year-old, a four-year-old, and a six-year-old. We would return six weeks later with two two-year-olds, two four-year-olds, and two six-year-olds. To say life was pure uncertainty for a while would be an understatement. Little in life is certain when you're parenting six kids under seven. The limited English language skills of our newest children added another layer to parenting, even though I speak some Luganda, the language most commonly used in the Ugandan region that was their home. In my preparenting days, I taught ESL; ESL parenting was another beast altogether. I didn't admit it to anyone at the time, but in that stretch of transition, even as I loved the children we'd brought home, I grieved the loss of our old lives, of everything familiar.

In our earliest weeks and months as a family of eight, when people asked how I was doing, I said something like, "Well, we're good when we can stick to a routine. But then each week, we've had something major: a snowstorm, the return of seizures for one kid, another snowstorm, colds for three kids followed by colds for two the next week and a cold for the last one the following week, and so on. Then the routine is lost, and I gain a couple pounds by stress eating until the next hopeful start to the week."

Every week, it was something. And every week, I started optimistically, until the something happened that dashed my hopes for the week. But about two months in, I had a realization that shifted my perspective.

I am a mom of six.

Of course, I already knew that, but acknowledging it helped. It clicked that as the mom of six, every week was guaranteed to have something come up. All of those somethings weren't interruptions to our lives or inconveniences to our routine. They *were* our lives. They *were* our routine. Especially given how young our kids were and how many had various diagnoses, interruptions weren't the enemy of normal. They were the normal. Uncertainty was where we lived. Those pesky somethings that came up each week didn't wreck the week, as I originally thought they did.

And then, once we were settled and life made sense and dream after dream was coming true, everything changed again. Lee died. I learned why it's called a broken heart. No, it's not just the metaphor of the heart as the center of feeling. When grief is deep and relentless, you feel literal pain in your chest.

I felt it all the time in the beginning. Now it comes and goes, never offering warning before it pounces. Somehow grief feels like both a predator and a friend, a thief and a companion. That's fitting, I suppose, because grief is all about the both/and realities.

I can both laugh about silly Christmas memories and hate that Lee will never be present in new ones. I'm glad I'm back in a liturgical tradition of faith because my soul needs the seasons of Advent and Lent. It needs the both/and, the already/but not yet. Jesus is coming, but he's not quite here. I need Good Friday, but Easter is trickier.

I believed in an afterlife in an intellectual sort of way before Lee died. Now all rational analysis is gone because I can't breathe without the hope that his life continues into eternity and mine will too. If I'm wrong, I don't want to know any different because surviving this depends on telling myself stories of heaven.

Imprecatory psalms are my jam right now too. While the language is more polished, in most of those psalms David sounds a lot like he's praying my common prayer of "What the actual fuck, God?" When Christians get uncomfortable about how open I am with my pain or question my raw expressions of lament, I know they haven't read their Bibles. Someday I'll make an assigned reading list for friends of grievers, a list to remind us that the cheerfulness of our cultural Christianity is more culture than Christianity.

Tonight is one of those nights when my chest literally hurts. I'll take a Xanax soon, but right now I'm breathing through the pain and letting myself feel it all. I know the only way is through it.

I also know that there's not going to be another side to reach in this life. There isn't an overcoming of his death. No light at the end of the tunnel offers the reward we want most. We're running the race, but we know it's one with no finish line.

Living with Lee gave me a safety net. I could fall into his arms, fall into the security of his income, fall into the love we shared. Now, I'm still on this tightrope of life, but without the comfort of knowing who I call if my car breaks down and who I list as my emergency contact. Friends are intermittently spotting me, but they can't be everywhere. Some nights I have to journey in the dark on my own.

I'm mixing so many metaphors in these sentences, but I'm not sorry. I just answered a call from my daughter's Big Brothers Big Sisters program, and I realized I didn't have it in me to carry on the conversation. I said, "I'm sorry. I can't do this right now. My husband died five months ago, and it's Christmas. I don't know when a good time will be, but I know it isn't one right now." Some weeks it feels like there isn't going to be a good time ever again.

It's awkward to say that I can't talk right now because 150ish days ago, a wave knocked my husband to the ground with enough force to break his neck, immediately paralyzing him and severing the nerves that control major bodily functions like breathing and blood flow. He wouldn't be declared dead until twenty-four hours later, but he was already mostly gone when I got to him on the beach. So, no, right now isn't the best time to talk.

When people ask what I need, my mind goes blank except for this: I need Lee back. But no one can give me that, so I don't say the words I think.

I'm crying more nowadays. I don't know if that's good or not. I think it just is.

It feels like gravity disappeared July 19 when he died. I was at home in him. We all were. And now all the properties of the world as we knew it are gone. We have to learn how to not float away from everything without his grounding force.

Typical metaphors fail. How do you express that you feel like you're drowning when your husband actually did? How do you talk about waves of grief knocking you down unexpectedly when literal waves doing that were the cause of death? How do you ever look at the beach or water the same way ever again?

I can't even consider wearing a bathing suit yet, maybe ever. I grew up in Florida; the beach was a second home of sorts, my backyard pool my first home. I swam competitively in high school and was goalie for the University of North Carolina's water polo team in college. I'm a water girl.

Correction: I was a water girl.

I don't know who or what I am anymore. I hurt. I've learned, as Lisa did before me, that surviving is the brave act of moving through the agony instead of self-destructing by denying it. This heart pain reminds me I'm alive and he's not.

That's all I know for sure.

PART II

CHOOSING YOUR VOICE
IS BRAVE

CHAPTER 3

POWERFUL WORDS

research shows
one adult
offering the words
"I believe you"
makes a world of difference
for an abused child,
for me,
those words never came
until I spoke them
as an adult
to the child
I once was

don't know what to say."

Those words were extended to me again and again in the second half of 2019. No one knows what to say to a thirty-seven-year-old widowed single mother of six. It's not their knowledge that's lacking, though. No, it's words that fail.

Words are my profession. I can say with confidence that no

words exist for freak accidents. Death is a cruel thief, and sometimes it even steals our capability to wrap words around an experience. It certainly did when Lee died.

We call horrific experiences "unspeakable." Sometimes that's because our society has deemed them inappropriate to discuss. Where that is true, we need the bold and brave among us to turn what has been labeled unspeakable into something speakable, albeit still horrific. Words have the power to cut through the horror.

Sometimes, though, the terrible unspeakable circumstances are beyond words. Sometimes pain is palpable, but expressions of it are lacking. So how do we use the power of words in the midst of the unimaginable?

My friend Rabbi Ruti Regan gave the best example in a tweet reply to me. She wrote, "For what it's worth, I'm not afraid of you or your grief and I don't need you to reassure me that things are okay that obviously aren't at all okay." These words hold power even when other words are wholly insufficient.

They remind me of what Lee would say when I shared a story of the evil done to me as a child. Words don't exist to respond adequately to the horrors I endured, so he would simply say, "Empathy," as his way of expressing that he was with me in everything, even this. That single word was his reminder to me that I have never been too much or not enough.

Sometimes a single word holds all the power you need. Sometimes an honest "I don't know what to say, but I am so sorry and you are so loved" speaks volumes. Sometimes it helps to put your own spin on a comforting phrase, as when my friend Lauren replied, "Fuck and empathy," to the news that Lee had died.

Sometimes the power of our words is more poignant in the moments in which we choose not to use any but instead to simply show up for one another. My friends Lindsey, Rachel, Amy, and Angie didn't say much when they joined me at the hospital as Lee was dying, but their presence spoke power enough. They made sure I knew that they could receive any words I had to say, giving me full permission to speak as much or as little as I needed.

No one knows what to say when a life shatters, and I was grateful for the friends who told the truth in their words and presence.

———

Rachel Held Evans taught me that my words were power. Hers sure were.

In one of our last exchanges before complications from the flu and an infection took her life far too young, she reminded me of something I want you to hear too. We were talking about a story she already knew well, when I lost both my job at my conservative church and my job at a Christian nonprofit in 2016 for being too politically and theologically liberal.

My boss at the nonprofit wrote, in a parting shot at me, that he wished me luck on "being the next Rachel Held Evans." Now, as I grieve the Rachel-size hole left in my world, I consider the comparison a precious compliment.

He certainly didn't mean it that way.

"Sounds like there are a million reasons not to listen to that guy," she started. Then she did what Rachel was known best for doing with newer writers. She encouraged me.

"I'm so glad you're here and you're YOU," she wrote. "I've learned so much from you these past couple of years. No doubt he meant it as an insult. But I see it as a compliment. I'd like to be more like you!"

Rachel was a treasure, and her memory and public words are a gift. Following her death, I saw calls for us all to be a little more like Rachel was. I didn't dispute any of them, because I agree the world would be a lovelier place with more Rachel in it. But I couldn't shake these words from our conversation three months before she died: *"I'm so glad you're here and you're YOU."*

I say the same to you right now. It's easy to default to the great writers or speakers of our past and present when we consider the power of our words. But you, reading this right now, are full of words that matter as much as mine or Rachel's do.

I'm so glad you're here. I'm so glad you're you.

———

Returning to that double job loss, wasn't 2016 a fun year politically? (No. No, it wasn't.)

I live in North Carolina. HB2 passed here in 2016. HB2 was our bathroom law stipulating that people use the toilets designated for the sex listed on their birth certificate. In North Carolina, the birth certificate piece made it even more challenging for trans folks because the only way to officially change assigned gender then was to do so postoperatively. Surgeries can be expensive and excruciating and inaccessible and undesired, so that provision assumes trans people aren't really trans unless their gender identity and bodily anatomy match.

I disagreed with the law on a fundamental level, but it was also entirely unenforceable without hiring and funding bathroom bouncers to check birth certificates at restroom entrances. I was furious. I wanted to rant. I have never been quiet on social media, but I was careful with what I posted. I knew what would happen if I wasn't. I had learned through tears with my friend Stephanie.

Stephanie had posted a photo collage on Facebook of her cousin's wedding a year earlier. That seems innocuous, right? She had been mentoring a group of teenagers at our church for years, but she wasn't allowed to go to camp with them or serve in any capacity with them after she shared that image, which showed her cousin and his husband kissing in a small corner of the collage. I didn't even notice that scene when I clicked that I loved it. Because she refused to delete the picture or add "I love my cousin, even though I don't agree with his homosexual lifestyle," she was effectively shunned. She didn't even get to say goodbye to the girls.

In the midst of that story, before she knew that she was done at our church, she texted me. I wasn't sure what was going on, but I said yes when she asked if she could stop by. She showed up with tears and confusion, not understanding why an innocent picture of a family wedding was turning into such a huge ordeal. She knew I was safe because I had clicked LIKE on her photo; no one else from our church had.

I didn't leave the church at that time. I understood why Stephanie did, but I was still naively confident I could shift the culture of the church from within. It's easy to vilify people who hold beliefs we abhor, but it's hard to keep the people and the beliefs separate. I didn't agree with their beliefs anymore, but I loved the people who held them. I loved God, and I loved people, and I believed it was best to sacrifice most of myself for that love.

So I stayed.

By the time HB2 rolled around, I was drained. I'd been the disability ministry coordinator there for almost a decade, yet our family ministry pastor sat across from me in one of our last meetings and said he really didn't consider the needs of disabled kids when he planned events, chose curriculum, or made other decisions. As a disabled mom with an autistic son and a wheelchair-using daughter, his words stung both personally and professionally. After depleting myself for love, I felt like I wasn't loved or even known in return.

Then HB2 passed.

I didn't dare post anything publicly until I met with the pastor. I was ready to explain how studying the Bible had led me to conclude that trans identity was entirely consistent with God's desires for our world. I was also ready to hear that I could no longer continue in my current position because our church had recently adopted a statement of belief labeling LGBTQ+ identity as a sin incompatible with God's design.

The conversation went both well and as expected. I left without my job. I didn't realize this yet, but I was also leaving that church. We never returned.

I spoke up because it was right to do so. I spoke up because I had the privilege to walk away if it came to that, because of my husband's income. I spoke up because silence made me feel like I was going to vomit.

More than anything, I spoke up because people matter. May we always use the power of our words to declare that to be true.

———

As we left our church of eleven years, I found solace in knowing I didn't leave ministry work altogether. No, I continued my side job as a consultant for a nonprofit, equipping churches to be radically inclusive of people of all abilities. I loved the work and the difference it made. My identity had been unhealthily wrapped up in ministry for so long that leaving my church would have undone me if I didn't still have a church-related job.

Then I wrote a naive post that would be called brave. The July 2016 blog's title was "I'm Pro-Life. And I'm Voting for Hillary. Here's Why." I don't consider it courageous because I genuinely didn't believe anyone would read anything on my relatively small blog, especially not a political post after years of avoiding politics. Sure, my words were called powerful as they were shared and as I was profiled by *The Wall Street Journal*, *Slate*, and *Daily Kos*. But it doesn't take much moxie to hit PUBLISH on an eight-thousand-word essay you think only four or five people, max, will ever read. (It's at two million reads at this point, something I never fathomed.)

I had never written about politics before. I didn't know the polarized responses I would get. I was with Clinton for the election, but my post wasn't meant to persuade the public as much as it was to make a few people ponder.

My personal blog wasn't connected with my job, but I was undeniably the most well-known of our consultant team. I didn't realize my writing outside of work would be problematic for anyone else. I should have. I definitely should have when my boss texted me, "Having fun counting your blog hits tonight?"

When Emma Green at *The Atlantic* covered this story as part of a larger piece on evangelical women who were fired or lost financial support because of their political beliefs, one sentence makes me laugh out loud every time: "As the summer drew to a close, though, it became clear that her political writing was a problem." That is a marvelous understatement. Within a couple of months of my blog post and the week before our family joined a new church—Methodist this time instead of Southern Baptist—I was given the option to quiet down about politics or resign.

By that conversation, I had learned the power of my words in a way I hadn't understood before. Finding my voice and facing the critics in the cheap seats hadn't come easy. I had millions of new readers, publishers were offering to turn my one post into a brand, and I didn't know what I wanted.

I did know, though, that my words were mine alone. I wasn't ready to give anyone else their power, and I didn't yet know how to use it myself. But I was determined to learn.

I resigned. In four months, I lost two jobs because my politics prioritized people forgotten by the American church. I didn't know what was next, but I knew I would use my words for whatever good I could.

———

So why do I do what I do in continually speaking out against inequity in our world? I could give you a line about how my black and Asian children have made me more compassionate and aware of the world in new ways, but that's not it. (They did, but so did my white children. Parenting can bring about more coming-of-age growth than adolescence.) That's not where it started for me. As a child, I devoured books about pain and injustice—from *A Little Princess* to Anne Frank's diary to *Roll of Thunder, Hear My Cry!*—because I connected most to them.

I had my fair share of pain and injustice, sure, but I also started life on third base already in other ways. While I've faced challenges aplenty, I've also been handed advantages that everyone deserves. When it comes to those of you who lack the privileges I had, I don't endeavor to speak for you, because you can choose when and how and if you tell your story, on your terms. You don't have to speak out to live brave. It's the living of the story, not the telling of the story, that makes you brave.

As I skim social media feeds this evening, powerful protests are popping up all over the world following George Floyd's death at the hands—well, the knee—of a white officer who used excessive and deadly force on a black man because of a counterfeit $20 bill. And I see some white people who are brazen enough to describe what it is to be black in this country while failing to highlight the work and words of those whose lived experiences tell a better story. I think they feel like it's easier or important to tell someone else's story for them, but doing so is also dehumanizing and infantilizing.

I know what it's like to suffer yet be unheard. That's the story of most abused children. I still had a voice, though. I still wanted to speak. I would rather have had someone invest in me and empower me to speak instead of pretending I was voiceless. In metaphorical terms, this is painful, but there was a more literal sticking point for me.

I was born with my arm wrapped around my head, which doctors said led to abnormalities in my vocal apparatus. I received special education speech services at school until sixth grade. I couldn't pronounce the sounds *s*, *sh*, *r*, *l*, *f*, and most vowels. My maiden name was Shannon Saunders. I struggled to even express my own identity, only able to articulate *nnn nd* from my name.

I suppose someone could have traveled with me to interpret all the time. That would have been nice at my brother's high school football game when I tried to order a Snickers bar but ended up crying alone behind the concessions stands without my candy. All I could say was *nck*.

I hated it at the time, but I grew from the struggle. I needed to fight to speak for myself. I needed a long-term plan and not just short-term solutions. I needed the speech therapists who guided me through learning how to speak. I needed the physical therapist who taught me to strengthen the muscles of my neck so I could hold my head high. I needed people to invest in me, not to speak for me.

Now, I speak clearly on my own. All people should be afforded the same dignity to communicate as they choose to do so, be it through words or art or assistive communication devices or signs. This includes being able to choose when and if they share their stories, because stories are sacred.

———

To drive home the point that any use of words involves risk of failure while also adding a bit of levity to a heavy chapter, here's the story of how I accidentally sent a picture of my vagina to all our closest friends and family. I wish that sentence was a metaphor. It isn't. It all happened the night our first child was born.

The pregnancy with her was rough. My body struggled through every trimester; I lost twenty pounds in the first because of severe morning sickness and spent the other two trying to keep my iron count within low-normal ranges. I loved the outcomes of my pregnancies with our two biological children, but the road to get there felt like it could crumble at any moment.

When I went into labor on her due date, I thought my hips were being torn apart from the inside out. When it was finally time to push, nineteen hours later, I started crying because I didn't think I could do it. I ended up with a third-degree tear in my perineum. That's the fancy medical term for the skin between the vulva and the anus. It felt just as marvelous as it sounds.

My mom took a sweet picture of my husband holding our daughter while I was being sewn up. I was probably on some impressive pain meds when I emailed it out to all our closest friends and family. My husband and I both failed to notice the doctor in the background with my lady parts reflected in the shield covering her face. One friend on our list, an ER doctor and a groomsman in our wedding, noticed the mistake, blurred that area, and sent the edited version back to us.

This also means he had to look closely to make the PG version. I try not to think about that.

To unravel any bit of dignity I had left, the room was also

full of people. The hospital had just gotten a new computer system, and everyone was learning. While my feet were in the stirrups and the OB was stitching me up, about ten people walked by my totally revealed everything.

Flashing my naked crotch to all my people in an emailed birth announcement didn't kill me, but I am glad I wasn't on social media yet. I wanted to take back the email, the words, the announcement, and, most of all, the picture. But just like our words when we put them out there, we don't always get to choose the consequences (especially when we've been clueless or under the influence of drugs, both true for me here, or if we've been thoughtless in other ways).

As I listen and act and care, I can't stay silent. That doesn't work for me. When I use my words, I'm going to fall flat on my face sometimes. I'll get my ass kicked sometimes, and some of those times I'll deserve it. I'll get myself up and dust myself off, or maybe I'll stop being so stubborn and let others help me.

I emailed a vag pic to everyone close to me, including my pastors and in-laws, but I'm not defined by that. Nor should any of the rest of us be for our most blush-worthy gaffes.

We'll misspeak and mess up, but the risk is worth it. We are more than our mistakes. Being brave can change the world, or at least our little corner of it. That's why I do what I do, even when it comes with a side of hate mail or accidentally X-rated images.

Sometimes we'll want to rewind the moment and get a second chance to better harness the power of our words, but life doesn't work that way. No, we take care with our words, knowing their potential, but we also carry with us the humility to own those words when we misfire.

In other words, I'm so glad you're here.

I'm so glad you're you.

And I'm so glad you haven't emailed a picture of your genitals to everyone you know.

CHAPTER 4

NOT KEEPING SECRETS

I stayed
silent
because I knew my own darkness
I wanted
to protect
those who hadn't experienced
the darkness I survived
from knowing the hard truths I faced
back to the sun
I didn't know
those who loved me
would rather enter the shadows
than leave me alone there

My personal shifts haven't been completely private, but the roots of them were hidden until the past few years. I'm going to tell it all here through the story of my knees, but you'll find that this is much more than that story. It's much more than my story, I'm realizing too. It's a story of how drowning doesn't look like drowning until it does.

My knees looked fine, as far as knees go. I'm not sure they're anyone's favorite body part. The function is helpful, but otherwise, they're just there, waiting to be skinned or to fail.

When my knees first failed, I was at an age at which they still wore childhood scabs. It wasn't supposed to be like that, but it was, all at the same time. By male family members, my body had not been my own for a long time, maybe ever, so nothing felt incongruous to me about my kneecaps being forcibly dislocated as my legs were spread against my will.

I was eleven.

I didn't tell anyone until I was fifteen because I didn't know how to say what happened without feeling like I was telling on myself. I knew what happened was wrong, but I didn't know I wasn't wrong along with it. I didn't know how to tell the story of my knees without confessing something primally disorienting. Daddies are meant to protect their young, but mine should have been a protector by trade too. He wore a badge, a uniform, and an officer's rank. Both our large metropolitan county's sheriff's office and our country's Green Berets in Vietnam knew him well.

So did my body.

At fifteen, my kneecaps finally dislocated in a public place, in the ordinary act of climbing in a van. Other people saw. They asked if it had ever happened before, and I said no. I still didn't know how to say yes. I still didn't know saying yes wouldn't be the same as saying I was a whore. I still didn't know if I could tell the truth that incestuous abuse had evolved into other men being invited into our home and my body without my consent, because I still didn't know that I wasn't complicit in my trafficking. I still didn't know the truth that none of it was my fault. My knees knew, though, and they told some of the story before my words could.

A condescending doctor dismissed me as my mother spoke over me, telling him this was a one-time incident when she and I both knew it wasn't. I went to physical therapy. I learned how to strengthen muscles to compensate for my injuries, which seemed about right. I had been compensating for injuries in secret my whole life, with my earliest memory being one of terror as I ran from physical danger in the form of a family member. I don't remember what happened after I got caught, and I think that's probably merciful.

I started to tell parts of the story, bit by bit. I earned a scholarship with an essay I had to recant once my mom found out I had written about the abuse. While the committee couldn't prove my original story was the truth without my cooperation, they still awarded me the honor. I imagine they thought they were helping, hoping to be guardian angels for a young woman in need of a legion, and they were.

In high school, I told my story by extreme perfectionism, not just trying to be perfect but needing to be to earn love and belonging. (I didn't know those were my birthright.) In college, I told my story with binge drinking and bulimia. Going back to age eleven, I told my story with thin lines carved into my forearms and upper thighs.

It was socially acceptable to be a perfectionist, a problem drinker, a sickly thin girl, and even a cutter. Being a teenager who had a decade of sexual and physical and emotional trauma behind her, while walking on knees that told a story that my lips couldn't? That wasn't anything anyone wanted to hear. It was socially acceptable to talk about the horrors of sex trafficking, but I noticed it was not socially acceptable to be a survivor of it. I knew no one who told that story, who told my story of being sold as a young teenager to be raped by strangers while my dad watched.

If they did tell that sort of story, it never included happy endings. It never included love. I never expected mine to include that either. (If I'm honest, the tragedy of July 2019 made more sense to me than the love stories of December 2000 until then.)

I didn't mean to fall in love. Lee was an accident. If I had seen him coming, I would have tried to protect myself by pushing him away.

Because he loved me, I started to believe that maybe I had never been in the wrong after all. I started sharing some of my childhood secrets. I started to see doctors who could hear parts of my story and treat injuries that should have been treated years before, injuries that should never have happened to need to be treated.

I knew how to do, so I kept doing. I didn't know how to be. I didn't know how to breathe. I didn't know how to rest. I didn't know how to care for a body that had known only neglect before Lee.

While he was alive, I rarely told others about my love story with Lee. It was ours, to be lived rather than told. I like to play a cynic but couldn't keep that up whenever I acknowledged how much of a fairy tale I entered when I met him. He wasn't perfect. I'm not perfect. Our life together wasn't perfect.

But somehow that didn't matter with him. It never did. But *I* always mattered to him, in a way I never knew I could matter before he happened to me.

Lee happened to me twenty years ago. Our fairy tale looked picturesque on the outside, as our stories weaved together into the lives of our children through birth and adoption in ways we hadn't expected. People fell in love with the idea of our family, and they couldn't see my gasping for air because they had placed me on a pedestal too far away to check my vitals. They wanted to see a happy ending, not a woman whose secrets were still smothering her. Oddly enough, I was better than ever before, but being better meant I could finally see the cracks, not that they were gone.

Even as I saw therapists and specialists and had a few corrective surgeries early in our marriage, I was still drowning on dry land. My knees had looked mostly fine. I still knew how to compensate, and I used that to downplay the increasing erosion of joint and spine function, as the years of violence stopped hiding below the surface, as my history met my present, as my body revealed it had been keeping score all along.

That's the story of unbecoming and becoming, not linearly but cyclically, that ushered me into the weirdness of these past few years. That's how I ended up having seven major surgeries between March 2017 and September 2018. That's how I ended up here, in such a different space than I used to be, even before Lee died. My personal weirdness happened to coincide with America's political farce of fact and fiction, and it was nice to collide with my internal reckoning while the rest of the world watched—and continues to watch—our country's collective external one. That's how I felt less alone.

Yes, politics plays a role in my unraveling from chaos into something still taking form today but not quite there yet. For me, it hasn't been the catalyst it has for so many others. Sure, I've written about the impact of presidential politics and partisan pandering, but for me, that's been the side story, not the central one.

Sometimes the sideshow distracts from the larger story. It has for many who have been following along with mine. And it reminds me of something I learned in my lifeguard training, not long after Lee and I met.

Drowning doesn't look like drowning until it does. The splashing and struggling isn't the danger. No, I blew my whistle for that to prevent injury, not to highlight any that had already occurred. Drowning—real drowning—looks like almost nothing at all. It isn't splashy. It is a slow slipping under, a gradual burial that isn't obvious until it's too late unless you know what to look for.

I've been un-drowning for a few years now, and breathing deeply without gulping down waves of misplaced blame, shame, and guilt still feels foreign. My knees are as fixed as they can be, but they had to be literally taken apart and reassembled through four surgeries. That part of the story, the surgeries and recoveries, has been visible. The part of the story in which my soul has done the same has been harder to see, mainly because it was never meant to be seen until now. It wasn't a secret anymore, but it was held private from those who aren't intricately woven into my life, at least not while the story's words were still being intimately crafted from wounds into scars. When Lee died and news outlets around the world told the story of our deepest grief, the pain was public for a change.

I'm not sure what has been more difficult: private pain or public tragedy. Both suck. I'd definitely prefer a third option.

Some of my longtime readers met me when I was drowning but looked dry. All the transition that's been happening in public and private has been cohesive in my larger narrative but probably confusing from the outside. Even questions like "Wait, another surgery? What in the world?" are ones that have been completely logical while also being heavier questions than they seem on the surface.

The heaviness of them, the years of unpacked "griefcases" underwater, was my iceberg, while the world only saw the exposed tip. As I've found my way to the surface, the unpacking of secrets has made me seem different from before.

And I am.

I used to think that was wrong. I valued consistency in viewpoints as if that were a sign of integrity. I've learned now that real integrity includes room for growth and change and learning and unpacking, of being somehow the same and yet completely different all at once.

Though our stories aren't identical, I imagine my words resonate with you. I'm not the only one experiencing this state of sameness to and difference from the person I once was. I know too that many others are drowning, just like I was, but it doesn't look like drowning, not yet. Because drowning never looks like drowning until it does.

I am not alone. You are not alone. Those who are drowning imperceptibly aren't alone either. We were each made not only to be human but also to be bound to one another in our shared humanity, none of us made less by our secrets.

The world seems like it's at least half ruined, but it felt that way when I was eleven too. Some of the ruin is still ruin, yes, but some of it has been redeemed into something like hope. If you're disoriented by all the differences or drowning in them, I'm here to let you know that the beautiful and horrible secret of life is that it always changes.

That change is inescapable, but the drowning doesn't have to be. We can figure out how to swim, not on our own but by learning from each other. It's been a weird few years, yes, but our griefcases full of secrets don't have to anchor us in sameness.

Drowning doesn't look like drowning until it does, after all, but drowning doesn't have to be inevitable.

———

"Why didn't you tell me when we were kids?" Hannah asked. It was a fair question. We were best friends, inseparable starting at age three and continuing through elementary school. Middle school was rough on our relationship, but we came back together in high school. We were bridesmaids in each other's weddings. Our lives have been woven together as long as I can remember.

She knew I was often scared to go home. She knew I had bruises from time to time, but she accepted whatever story I offered to explain them. She knew I knew more about sex than she did at an early age. She knew I lied often, but she didn't understand that it was a defense mechanism because the truth was too hard to speak. She knew I spent as much time as I could at her house. She knew I loved to read, but she never knew I did it all the time because it was one of my only escapes from a world no writer could conjure.

But until we stood outside that pool hall the summer before my wedding, Hannah didn't know the secrets that had been killing me. She didn't know about the rapes or sex trafficking. She didn't know I attempted suicide at age eleven. She didn't know about the self-harm or disordered eating. She knew our relationship was strained through those years, but she didn't know it was because I wanted to protect her from the horrors I was living.

The truth is I didn't want to tell her. I wanted it all to stop, just as every abused child wants their pain to end. But I loved my family. I didn't want them to get in trouble, even though they would have been arrested, most likely, if my dad hadn't been so influential in local law enforcement. I was worried about something else too, something other than the criminal charges they deserved.

A precocious child, I read the newspaper cover to cover beginning at age seven while sitting across the kitchen bar from my dad. I started with science and lifestyle features, but soon I was reading it all. I remembered the stories of foster children being abused or even killed in the homes in which they were placed. I knew how to navigate the abuse of my own home, and I was scared I might not be able to handle a different kind of abuse.

More than anything, though, I felt like I was keeping a secret about myself, not about what they did to me. I was brainwashed by their verbal, physical, sexual, and spiritual abuse. I was convinced that if I could just be a better student, a better athlete, a better volunteer, a better person, a better Christian, and a better daughter, then the abuse would stop. I genuinely believed that if I could be enough, more enough than I was, then I wouldn't get raped anymore.

I couldn't know then how wrong I was about that. All I knew was I thought less of myself because of their crimes, so I was sure other people would feel the same way. The truth would have damned them, but I was sure it would be damning for me too. If I spilled my secrets, I thought I'd also be sharing how little I was worth. I was certain some error in the core of who I was conjured up all the pain. After all, I thought, if my parents and older brother wouldn't or couldn't love me like a daughter or sister should be loved, then maybe there was something undeserving of love in me.

So I told no one. Once I began talking about the physical abuse, I kept the other cards close to my chest, hiding the stories that happened in beds. Middle school girls want to be known but they usually don't want to be too different from their peers. I knew my torture would set me apart in a way I didn't want, probably drawing pity at the same time.

No, thank you.

On any other topic in life, Hannah and I told each other every detail. She knew about my first consensual kiss. I knew about her crushes. She knew about the time I peed in our favorite tree by accident and lied about it. I knew about the time she fell in the lake and tried to dry off before going home so her parents wouldn't suspect anything. (They were more attentive than mine, so they caught on immediately. We weren't as stealthy as we thought.) We knew about each other's first periods, least favorite teachers, hopes for the future, and questions about God's existence, though we always said "dog backwards" because we didn't want her parents to hear us and think we were taking the Lord's name in vain.

But she never knew the secrets held behind my front door. I figured she'd ask if she wanted to know. She assumed I'd tell if there was anything worth telling. During the most painful and violating stretch in middle school, I lost the skill of pretending for a while, at least pretending with my dearest and longest-held friend, so I avoided her. In a scrapbook of our childhood pictures she gave me when we were in our early twenties, she wrote this about those years: "I don't have many pictures of us from middle school. I think maybe we were fighting a lot then." Even our picture albums screamed that something had been off, even if she never knew what it was. Her childhood was safe and secure, so she thought mine was too. She had no way of suspecting that my secrets were sucking life from me.

I couldn't let her know it all because I tried to pretend I didn't know any of it. I tried to convince myself that abuse out of sight was out of mind. I looked okay to my best friend, but I was imploding inside, internally manifesting the words of Bessel van der Kolk: "As long as you keep secrets and suppress information, you are fundamentally at war with yourself. . . . The critical issue is allowing yourself to know what you know. That takes an enormous amount of courage."[4]

Back then, it took all the courage in me to stay alive. It would take many more years to let myself not only know what I knew but say it out loud to a friend. I'm still working on putting my weapons down, calling a truce to the war I've long fought with myself.

———

My childhood taught me that we all have inner and outer lives. As a family, our outer lives were ones of influence and wealth and privilege. Our inner lives were full of mental illness and secrets of abuse. That contrast is more drastic than most, but we all do this.

Our inner lives are who we are, drenched in authenticity. Our outer lives are who we think we should be, a character of our own design. The idol my parents held dearest was the perfect family. We weren't that, by a long shot, but they wanted people to think we were. Bruises needed to be covered. Injuries hidden. Fights ended as soon as we stepped out the front door. Mom wore titles of PTA president at the school and later secretary at the church, while I wore slaps to my face at home and contusions under my clothes. I heard "Isn't your dad amazing?" when we were out of the house, while I was forced to sit and comply in his lap with porn on the television when no one else was around. I was sacrificed on their altar of perfection.

It's no wonder my favorite holiday was Halloween. I was pretending to be someone else every day of my life. My costume was that of the happy daughter in a perfect family. I knew it was all facade, but I didn't know how to do anything else. Maybe if I put on the show they wanted, then I would earn the right to be loved at home, I thought.

Halloween was the one day out of the year when everyone else pretended too. Nice girls could be witches. Nerds could dress up as football players. Being scared was fun on Halloween, we all agreed, but no one knew I was scared every day. On October 31, I could use face paint over any bruises I would usually hide by letting my hair fall over the shades of purple, red, green, and yellow on my cheek. For one night of every year, the rest of the world knew I was pretending. They were clueless all the other days.

That night, I could slip into a character for the rest of the evening. Once I was a 1920s flapper, complete with blue fringe and a sequin headband. Another year I was Figment, the dragon from Epcot's Journey into Imagination. I still have a Juliet dress I wore one year, a Belle costume from another year, and a Cat-woman mask. When I was fourteen, I wore a chicken suit with bright orange tights. My favorite year was when I dressed up as Maleficent, my all-time favorite villain decades before she was popularized by Angelina Jolie on the big screen and Disney's Descendants franchise on cable TV.

I look back more fondly on those nights than on any of the days I spent pretending in between. I chose to pretend on Halloween. I chose my role. I chose my story. I could take off my costume at any moment and be done with it.

My other costume, that of the loved daughter in a perfect family, hurt me. It was heavy with secrets that suffocated. When I went into acting for a while, that gave me more days to pretend by choice than just October 31. But every curtain call, like every November 1, I had to go back to being me. And being me as a child was exhausting. I didn't even like me. I would rather pretend I didn't care. I tried to perfect apathy, but inside I was screaming like Harry did at Dumbledore in *Harry Potter and the Order of the Phoenix*:

"I DON'T CARE!" Harry yelled at them, snatching up a lunascope and throwing it into the fireplace. "I'VE HAD ENOUGH, I'VE SEEN ENOUGH, I WANT OUT, I WANT IT TO END, I DON'T CARE ANYMORE!"

"You do care," said Dumbledore. He had not flinched or made a single move to stop Harry demolishing his office.

His expression was calm, almost detached. "You care so much you feel as though you will bleed to death with the pain of it."[5]

My screams were silent, though. No one heard. No Dumbledore met me with harsh honesty or blunt empathy. I was left pretending, while I was suffocating with the pain of it.

———

Mine is a story of resilience, but none of us earns survival like a merit badge. No, while badassery is a component, resilience requires outside help. The very fabric of surviving reminds us that we were made for connection rather than isolation.

We talk about childhood as formative years for a reason. They form us. When malformative pressures like abuse, trauma, and chronic stress are present, kids are hurt, sometimes for a moment, for a season, or for a lifetime. As for me, managing PTSD and reducing symptoms is a therapeutic goal, but the severity of my trauma means its imprint will always be with me, much like Harry's lightning-shaped scar.

For any of us to survive trauma, we need some hope dealers in our lives. Psych textbooks call them "protective factors," but I haven't liked that language since I first met it as a precocious kid tucked in the corner of the public library where no one would notice a ten-year-old reading a heavy trauma text. The people and things infusing hope into my life might have protected me from many long-term repercussions of abuse, but they rarely protected me in the sense I wanted. When I read the words "protective factors," I imagined a bubble around me, like a hamster ball, keeping all unwanted touches away. I would have loved that, but it never came.

I did have Bev and Jeff, a couple in whom I found refuge as I babysat for their kids and lobbied successfully to spend the night more often than necessary. I had the library, where trauma research taught me I wasn't alone. For me, school was safe. The rules of school made sense. I was smart, the sort of kid who didn't have to study and who speed-read through books like they were air to breathe. My academic excellence resulted in acceptance to colleges far from home, which were the same sort of reprieve that Harry's invitation to Platform 9 3/4 turned out to be. The University of North Carolina was my Hogwarts, minus any Voldemort.

All survival tools aren't protective, though. My working definition of "resilience" is the badassery of surviving and healing. I include both surviving and healing because they are different. Sure, there's some overlap. But just like a hamster ball would have helped me survive by keeping out unwanted touch, it would have prevented healing by keeping away those who were safe. Survival is getting from point A to point B on a timeline. Healing, on the other hand, requires relationship. When the idea of safety is destroyed for a child (or maybe never existed), survival can get them through, but healing—that is, recreating the ability to feel safe again—takes trust and truth, as we'll explore in the next chapter.

The groundwork for healing is that of mindfulness. Being mindful is the act of noticing without judgment. Where are you? Notice that. What can you see? Notice that. What can you hear? Notice that. What can you smell? Notice that. What can you taste? Notice that. What can you touch? Notice that. How does your body feel? Is it hot, cold, sweaty, calm, jittery, in pain, something else? Notice all these things, but don't judge your body or bodily responses as acceptable or unacceptable. What feelings are rising in you about any of these present realities? Notice those, but don't judge your emotions as good or bad. What things can you control? Notice those. What is outside of your circle of control but still something within your circle of concern? In other words, what are those things you can't control but that still evoke a sense of concern or care within you? Notice those.

To be mindful, you must notice without judgment, but you also must stay in the present moment. Where are you now? What can you see now? What can you touch now? Being grounded in the here and now brings life into focus. Rather than the complex but unchangeable stories of our past or the breadth of possibilities for the future, the present is finite. Fix yourself there.

That's where healing starts. Now. Here.

CHAPTER 5

HARD TRUTHS

I'm learning to befriend the flashbacks
as teachers
as reminders
as remembrances
as commemorations
of the hell I endured to get here
of the harm that failed to break me
of the healing I fought agony to find
of the high value of
my heart
my soul
my mind
my spirit
even as those weren't treated with dignity
even as touches and words couldn't be undone
even as I began to speak to myself
with the hatred
with the evil
with the abuse
they showed me for so long

I hate what happened to me
but I cannot hate every flashback
because now I am safe
because now I know my worth
because now I see who triumphed
(and it.
was.
not.
them.)
this is radical acceptance

ee is dead.
Tomorrow Lee will still be dead.

That day in the future, the one that platitudes promise will be better, will still be a day when Lee is dead.

Not only do we try to hide death itself or any possibility of death behind a heavy curtain, but we also try to hide it with our language. People flinch when I say my husband is dead, but I'm not going to soften the hard truth with obscuring words to make others more comfortable with my grief. No, he didn't transition. He didn't pass away. He didn't leave. He isn't late.

He died.

He's dead.

This is a constant in my life.

If you prefer other language for your loved ones, if that makes grief easier to carry, then go for it. For me, though, it feels like we're trying to tuck the trauma into a warm bed and dress it up in the morning. Trauma is real, and it doesn't come with tidy bows. Trauma shows up in pain and aches and autoimmune diseases and panic attacks and avoidance and substance abuse and a million paths, most with hard endings if we deny trauma's hard truths.

I don't love trauma, but I know she'll be my sidekick for the rest of this life because trauma doesn't leave. She might sleep, but she wakes easily. I'm a young widow, a survivor of childhood abuse and teenage sex trafficking, a woman disabled by injuries sustained during that violence, a badass with PTSD who parents children who also know trauma intimately, a Christian who struggles to show up to my current (safe) church because of the hurt I've experienced in past ones, and a person with several chronic illnesses and what seems like miles of surgical scars if laid end to end. Healing can and does happen, but it's slow and unlikely to be complete in this life.

These parts of my story are ones to be owned, not erased. The pain of it all doesn't fade if we hide it like a dirty secret. Trauma does not define me, but it doesn't leave me either.

Lee is dead, and he will still be dead tomorrow.

———

The intro to this chapter might feel unsettling to you. It might not sit well in your soul. It might seem like it needs fixing.

It doesn't.

Grief, when acknowledged, is messy and invasive and disorienting. Culturally in the US, we avoid or sanitize pain. We don't know how to sit with it. Colonialization led to the stiff-lipped European settlers writing and reinforcing emotion-suppressing rules, while the interpersonally connected indigenous tribes were targeted for displacement and genocide. (My ancestors are included among those European settlers, the ones who actively advocated for the murder of Native Americans. I share that not out of guilt but because we can't improve the present while denying the past. This is part of my story and America's story, a hard truth that requires examination, the making of amends, and a larger table if we want to travel in a better direction.)

The hard truth about hard truths is that we can't learn them until we're willing to dwell in discomfort and even darkness by their side. The good news, though, is that we don't have to do it alone.

I was alone, though, in June 2009, with a newborn and a two-year-old, while my husband was deployed by the state's urban search and rescue (USAR) team to respond to a Slim Jim plant explosion. I was proud of him, but I was also struggling. Both/and.

Most folks are surprised to hear Lee was a first responder for some situations. He was an adorably nerdy engineer who didn't wear a uniform, unless you count chinos and a button-down shirt as a uniform. But when some disasters occur, firefighters and other first responders need engineers to help them shore up buildings or other structures to make sure the rescuers don't end up needing to be rescued. Usually, he only worked on disasters in our state, but he also consulted with the federal government after explosions in Mississippi, Florida, and Hawaii.

Of course, these disasters were never planned. Disasters never are. Hard truths are embodied in disasters.

As a result of that Slim Jim explosion, Lee never ate processed beef jerky again. I never considered it a real food, but my husband was the proud owner of the *A Man, a Can, a Plan* cookbook before we got married. Processed food didn't make him flinch even a little. But from that moment to the day he died, jerky was a nope, no way, no thank you.

We would laugh about that, but other losses that day were no joking matter. By the time USAR was on the ground, every survivor was already out. They didn't know that hard truth yet. It wouldn't have changed anything if they did.

Their job is rescue or recovery. "Rescue" is in their name because that's the outcome everyone prefers. It's the word used when living people are brought out of a disaster area. Recovery, on the other hand, is about bodies, dead yet still sacred bodies. More often than not, USAR can't know if it'll be a rescue or a recovery until they get in there. For the sake of victims at any scene and for the sake of my tenderhearted husband, I hoped he would never have to do any recovery. But he did that week in June, spanning both my twenty-seventh birthday and our fourth wedding anniversary.

I held everything down at home while Lee left for the site, with no idea when he'd return. Upon arrival, Lee pulled on his hazmat suit, with an oxygen tank, and went in, along with a firefighter. They searched area by area, through the night, with naps in between. Then he and his partner found her, one of the women who didn't survive. Lee knew her name. We read news stories about her life afterward. He talked about that day with his therapist. But otherwise, he kept it tucked away.

Few people, even close friends, know this story. It's like the unspoken rule I learned young as the daughter of a mentally unwell Vietnam veteran: you don't ask a soldier if he's killed anyone. For this particular story, it's been a mix of two other factors as well. Lee was fiercely protective of others, especially me and our kids. He felt the same way about the woman whose body he recovered. I'm not sharing her name either. Before his death, Lee agreed to allow me to share this story. I protect her identity because that's the only thing we can rescue, not so much for her as for her family.

But there's another reason no one asks for those details. We've conditioned ourselves in the United States to look at car crashes on the roadside and crime scenes on any of a few dozen crime shows, but we don't want to get close. We love to read stories of those who have survived horrendous situations and lived to tell the tale, but we're much less likely to enter into the mess with those who are still in the pain. When we do enter in, we're fixers. We want to make it better. We struggle to hold space for each other. As creatures of comfort, we pretty much suck at dwelling in discomfort, be it our own or someone else's. When it's too much, we look away. When we don't know what to say, we don't say anything. When a family experiences a crisis, we bring meals in the immediate aftermath, but then we slink away. Simply put, we do well with resolution and happily-ever-afters; we're not so keen on grief and not-yets.

To live brave, we have to learn new ways. We have to learn to accept uncertainty not as an aberration but as a natural part of life and humanity. We have to learn to sit with pain without trying to cover it up with platitudes or turning away simply because we have the privilege to do so.

I didn't craft any of these words flippantly. Right now, as I write this, I'm in week thirteen of COVID-19 quarantine with my six children and no adults other than our nineteen-year-old home health provider for my youngest child, provided through a Medicaid waiver program. The world is protesting police brutality as white supremacists show up with violence, some of them wearing law enforcement uniforms and some not. Nothing is certain, and each of my words here is weighed down with deep truth because that's all I have to offer in this present uncertainty.

Hard truths abound, and we can only survive them. But remember, surviving is brave, so we can do this.

———

Being a survivor of sexual assault bears the hard truth that any #metoo allegations feel a little bit personal. I hear the same questions: Why the allegations now? Why didn't she say she was raped back when it happened? How can we believe her?

And? It feels like they're talking about me, questioning my decisions, doubting the horror I lived.

My rapes were very real. My rapists live free. No charges were ever filed. I tried to tell some adults in my life back when rapes were as common as homework, but they didn't want to hear it. That's why, for decades, I tried to pretend what happened to me didn't matter. Doesn't matter. But it did. And it does.

Even if allegations are never voiced, they bubble up in other ways. Perfectionism. Promiscuity. Alcoholism. Depression. Repeated abusive relationships. Self-injury. Drug abuse. Suicide attempts. After all, the pain has to go somewhere.

And healing? Healing from sexual assault is a lot like a prolonged version of pouring hydrogen peroxide on a wound. Sure, it cleans out the dirt and debris and other unhealthy gunk, but it hurts like hell in the process. And it doesn't mean a scar won't be left behind.

When I wrote about rape allegations involving a presidential candidate in October 2016, the chorus of accusation-questioning and victim-blaming began. I had been following the case for months, but I didn't post about it initially because I couldn't bear to read these sorts of comments:

Why didn't she come forward sooner?

Doesn't this seem opportunistic?

Who is paying her to say these things?

When someone accuses another of robbery, we don't see these questions. We don't ask what they were wearing, why they were hanging out with the types of people who rob others, if they said no clearly. . . . No, we understand that it's a violation when someone steals someone else's wallet.

But when a man violates the body of a woman, all of a sudden her credibility is the primary concern. (Or his or theirs. I write from my experiences as a woman, but that doesn't erase the reality that men, especially trans men, and nonbinary people also survive sexual assaults.) The lessons start early, not in watching political hearings but in adult reactions to children.

When I was in elementary school and a boy from my speech therapy group grabbed my hand and put it on his crotch? I was told I shouldn't have been on the corner of the playground where adults couldn't see well, the implication being that my location stripped me of the right to be safe from sexual harassment.

When I was in sixth grade and a boy on my bus rubbed his hand on my rear and between my legs as I walked by? I was told I needed to sit closer to the front of the bus so he wouldn't be tempted, the implication being that I somehow asked for the attention as I walked by.

When I was in eighth grade and was caught kissing my boyfriend in the schoolyard after the final bell? The teacher lectured me about how I should have known better without saying a word to the boy, the implication being that boys will be boys but girls must be better.

When I was in high school and went to my friends' youth group? I heard lessons on sexual purity about how guys are visual creatures so it's the responsibility of young ladies not to be teases who lead them on, the implication being that if anything happened sexually—with or without consent—the girl was to blame.

And those lessons don't include the words said to me by an adult when I was four, after the first time I was molested: "How did you let this happen? Things like this don't happen to good girls."

And those lessons don't include what I learned with each rape: your body can be taken from you at any moment.

These lessons, they're taught young. They make up rape culture. And they don't even include the comments we read about victims, the questions about credibility, the way the victim is put on trial as much as the offender. This misplaced blame grows into something more insidious: shame.

Truth says what happened to you was disgusting. Shame says you're disgusting because of what happened to you.

Truth says this is one part of your life story. Shame says this defines your life story.

Truth says even when trauma was caused in the context of a relationship, healing is found in relationship too. Shame says no one can ever know what happened and still love you.

Truth says the offender did a bad thing. Shame says you, as the victim, are a bad thing.

Why don't women come forward earlier? Because speaking truth is hard, and because shame runs deep. Because investigations include invasive exams that are often retraumatizing. Because sharing the details of what happened to me with Lee and my therapist was hard enough, but doing so with officers and lawyers and other strangers makes me want to throw up. Because justice might be no jail time at all or such a measly sentence that it feels like a whole 'nother assault. Because sexual predators often seek out kids and adults who lack the internal and external supports to fight back, both during the assault and afterward.

Fighting shame and speaking truth require others. We can't do it alone. My people—my husband before he died and my therapist and close friends who believe me and believe in me—are God's ambassadors to my hurting heart when I'm swallowed by the pain of my past. But everyone doesn't have people like mine. And that's part of why every victim doesn't become a survivor. Suicide, overdose, homicide, and so on . . . that's the end of too many of our stories, far more statistically than the general population.

So why didn't one victim or another come forward before now? I don't know her exact reasons. I do know mine. But honestly, I think we should all be amazed—given our culture—that any victims ever come forward instead of questioning those who do.

———

In every other way but criminal or civil charges, I have spoken my hard truths publicly. That's the right choice for me, but please remember that speaking out isn't what makes us brave; living in the after is brave all by itself.

I'm often asked, though, why I haven't named names when it comes to those who committed sex crimes against me. After all, these are men who violated me in grotesque and horrific ways. Some of the assaults have no statute of limitations, per Florida law, because I was younger than twelve with offenders older than eighteen. I could still press charges against one of them, possibly others.

But I haven't, and I don't think I will.

The rates of conviction in sexual assault cases are low, but that's not why. Even if I were guaranteed a conviction, my skin crawls at the idea of having my past and my present probed in the ways pressing charges would involve. Just as it was for Dr. Christine Blasey Ford and Professor Anita Hill in the hearings following the sexual assault allegations against Brett Kavanaugh and sexual harassment ones against Clarence Thomas, respectively, the whole process would be retraumatizing. Like them, it would impact my entire family, and I am fiercely protective of my children, especially since their father's death. I do keep tabs on them from afar, willing to be as brave as Professor Hill and Dr. Blasey Ford if the need arises, but for now I'm choosing the brave that says, "I am whole and healthy and well, and this is what's best for me."

I got enough of a glimpse of what naming names and potentially pressing charges might look like when I filed a sexual harassment grievance as a twenty-two-year-old teacher against one of the administrators at my school. I was always on edge. People were whispering about me. I didn't sleep. I jumped at small noises. I spent some nights at a friend's house, frightened to be alone.

I know from experience that speaking the truth about trauma can end up as a new trauma by itself. And it's okay to protect yourself from future trauma.

I'll close out this chapter with a story of not sharing some hard truths with the world, because saying no to something can be just as brave as saying yes, especially when people say things like "But it could happen to someone else if you don't . . ." Hard no to that. It could happen to someone else if the criminals do it again. It is not my fault if they commit more crimes. I've been brave in the sharing and the not sharing, and you can be brave in whatever is best for you.

I acted after only a year of sexual assaults and harassment from my boss. Meanwhile I stayed in contact with all my family and endured their verbal abuse for decades and still choose not to name them. I was trying to forgive and forget with my rapists, hoping to—as Bible study leaders recommended to me—evangelize to them with my kindness, that it might lead them to repentance. (Spoiler alert: It didn't.) I didn't want to upset anyone. I was so used to bearing the pain in my family that I didn't realize I'd been carrying it far too long.

Rumi wrote, "Why do you stay in prison when the door is so wide open?"[6] For me, it was because the prison was all I knew. My eyes were accustomed to the dark, and I feared the light would burn my eyes. I'd even try to close the door sometimes. Sure, I was locked in, but everyone else was locked out. That was lonely, but it felt safe.

I didn't know there was any option but prison. The door was open, but I was sure it led to another prison. After all, if I filed a grievance, that created a prison of ostracization and property damage. If I said nothing, I had to endure continued abuse from my boss, and it was already escalating.

It was no different than the pattern I learned as a child. Break the family rules by naming what I survived at home, and I'd be on my own. Play along, and I'd keep emotionally bleeding out.

Everything felt like a prison.

The hard truth as a child was that I didn't have the key to open the cell door. As a new teacher, I had friends who helped me find a key within myself. The hard truth then was that I didn't know what life could be outside of a cage.

That's the hard truth of freedom. It will always involve risk and often come with consequences. I decided the uncertainty of freedom was worth whatever might happen after turning the key.

Both freedom and captivity are unsafe in their own ways.

When we're captive, all we know is imprisonment. When we look toward freedom, it's all unknown.

The hardest truth is that no path is guaranteed to be safe. We move through the world with that knowledge. That's hard, and it's true.

And that's why we need to be brave.

PART III

TRUSTING IS BRAVE

CHAPTER 6

KEEPING THE FAITH (SOMETIMES BY LOSING IT)

I am not pulled together
but
I am not broken
I'm recovering
owning all the disinherited
parts of my story
and stitching the pieces
together with gentle threads
and finding beauty in
the scraps strewn on the floor
as I come together with myself into
all my Creator intended
for me

Full disclosure: I'm pissed at God.

I show up to church. Yesterday morning we sang a song with the line, "Lord, you are good, and your mercies endureth forever," and I stayed seated. I might be up for acknowledging

God's goodness in a cheery song someday, but yesterday was not that day. Today isn't either. Don't hold your breath—that day isn't coming anytime soon.

It might come when I least expect it.

It might not come at all.

And? It's okay if it doesn't. God can handle my anger. If I believe I'm created in the image of God, then I have to believe nothing about me is a surprise to my Creator.

Nothing about me (or you) is too much. My faith is like manna right now, only enough for each day, sometimes not quite enough to make it through bedtime.

On those days, I do like I did during the song in church: I close my eyes. I trust that the faith of my community is sufficient when the faith of my core is absent.

I let myself be still in that knowledge. I let myself be pissed in that knowledge. No matter where I am, I let myself be me in that knowledge, trusting that I am enough and God is more than enough for whatever might come.

———

My life has been saturated with pain, even before my husband died. Once I've told my story in full, I'm often asked, "But wait . . . how can you possibly believe in God after all that?"

Short answer: I do, but I'm not sure I can explain it.

I am a person of faith. I don't believe, though, that faith is a choice. At the base level, it doesn't make sense. Who of us would choose this? No one. But faith works because I think it's a gift rather than a choice. As a Christian, I consider that gift to be given by the Holy Spirit. I'm not really sure how it works for other faiths, but it strikes me as similar. And agnostics and atheists, maybe you're the only reasonable ones here.

I had faith as a child. Given my childhood, it's illogical. Believing in an all-powerful, all-knowing, and always-present God while experiencing abuse by the hands and voices and genitals of others seems incongruous. A line in the play *J.B.: A Play in Verse* always comes to mind when I think of this: "If God is God, he is not good. If God is good, he is not God."[7] The point was that if God is in control of everything and we know bad things happen, then God can't really be good. Conversely, if God is good, then "he's got the whole world in his hands" sounds like bullshit because bad things seem out of place in good hands.

I never bought that, though.

Math wasn't my favorite subject in school, but I excelled in it, especially algebra. As I figured, there had to be an X factor. We live in the problems, as they're playing out. We know some variables. Others are shrouded in mystery. That's where faith arrives for me. Faith says, "I don't understand why life is what it is, at least not right now, but I'm going to trust that maybe there's something I'm not seeing."

I do think some things just happen because we live in a messed-up world in which all of us have free will. Every single one of us is both beautiful and brutal, both powerful and needy, both courageous and fallible. I hurt others sometimes.

Sometimes I get hurt by others. Sometimes both happen in a single moment. Other times our bodies fail us, and I don't believe in "everything happens for a reason." That smacks of our desire for certainty and our discomfort with "I don't know." Sometimes, I believe, shit just happens. How we respond always matters more than why it happened in the first place.

From a young age, the concept of divinity just made sense to me. I explored nature and felt a spiritual spark that convinced me a creator was responsible. I went to church with my family, who mostly attended for social reasons, but the rhythms of liturgy, of three passages of scripture read aloud, of communion, of singing together, and of passing the peace drew me in. I was often an acolyte, the kid who carries in the flame and lights the candles on the altar at the start of the service, and even if I had been raped the night before, there was something like hope in that flickering light. When visible and invisible wounds formed on and in me by abuse, the only way I could keep from utter despair was to believe in something better, in this world and the world to come. I began reading the Bible cover to cover regularly in hopes of finding answers. I only found more questions, but they elicited peace and trust in God for me as I lived in a house whose inhabitants were neither peaceful nor trustworthy.

Even in periods in which I'm not writing much, I know deep in my soul that I'm a writer. Even when I'm binge-watching Netflix instead of cracking a book, I know that I'm a reader.

Even after my first child died by a late miscarriage, I knew that I was and had been a mother, albeit of a child who never breathed out of the womb.

In the same way, even when so much of my childhood and this world feels godforsaken, I've always known, deep in me, a God story.

Sometimes I hate the church. Sometimes it feels like the church hates me. Sometimes I think people who have left the church make far more sense than those of us who have stayed.

Lisa is one who has left. She isn't so sure about God anymore. That makes sense to me. I'm not sure I would be either if I were her.

We met through the church as teenagers, both as youth representatives in the Florida-Bahamas synod of our branch of the Lutheran church. We were two of the only teenagers present at adult events, so even if we hadn't connected, we would have been friends by default. Everyone else was twenty years older than us. (As I write this, I'm twenty years older than that teenage version of myself, ancient by my standards back then.)

Through email and then social media we stayed in touch after I left for college in North Carolina. She was the one who christened me with the nickname Shannon Anna Dingle Heimer Schmidt when I met and started dating Lee. By the spring of 2015, Lisa and I had eight kids between us. By the end of that summer, we'd have one less.

When Eli was little, Lisa wrote this on their family's blog:

"The work I do matters because I do it for the Lord. I am in the spot where He has placed me. The diapers, the driving to and from school, the coaxing into the car seat, the reading the same book fifteen times in a row, the 'watch me make a basket,' the listening, the not snapping (or trying really, really hard and still snapping anyway), it all matters, even when it feels insignificant in the moment."

By 2015, Lisa longed for the moments that felt insignificant. Eli was sick. We didn't know if he'd get better. He didn't. It was an honor to proofread his obituary for the family, but I hate obituaries for four-year-old boys. I wish we didn't live in a world that requires them. I wish we didn't live in a world that requires pint-size coffins. I wish we didn't live in a world that requires Lisa to have any days without Eli.

The idea of God, of heaven, of any sort of practical theology is too intangible for Lisa. When she announced Eli's death online, she used these inspired words: "One of Eli's great gifts was that he pulled back the corners of people's hearts to the possibility of Love. If Eli swept out any cobwebs or cracked open a part of you that you had shut a long time ago, please leave it open. For Eli." And she lived that by showing up and lavishing love (and dark humor) when my Lee died exactly four years, to the day, after Eli did.

That's the sort of faith Lisa has now: a faith in the possibility of love. The possibility of God? Lisa isn't so sure about that.

Some days, especially those days when reminders of Eli and Lee are everywhere, I'm not so sure about God either.

———

Bibles were plentiful in my childhood home, but I rarely saw them open. Magazines were always around, though, the pages well-worn with food stains and folded pages and perfume samples torn out.

I don't read magazines regularly anymore. Sometimes I forget that and subscribe to something, just so it can take a trip to get to me, rest a little while on the coffee table, and then find a home in the recycling bin so it can be remade into something that will hopefully be read by the next person.

But I love taking a look at what's there in the checkout line or the waiting room. Now it's mostly tabloids and entertainment, with an occasional *Real Simple* or *TIME*. When I grew up, more of them were about the home: *Southern Living. Country Living. Coastal Living.*

Maybe it's because I've lived my whole life in the American South, but those magazine titles call forth warm, cozy feelings of serenity in style, cooking, and home decor. As a little girl, they spoke to me of what expectations I should hold for the future. Sure, they're romanticized (how is it that toys are rarely visible in any of the homes, even when small children are present?), but each offers an idealized image that's engaging enough for me to buy one occasionally.

There's one kind of living that will never be in the title or on the front page of any magazine trying to draw in readers: furnace living. No one asks for that. A furnace might help with warmth, but none of us really want to hang out there.

Daniel 3 has always been a favorite chapter of mine from the Prophets. If you're unfamiliar with it, it's a story of three men choosing God over the danger of an earthly king's threats of death. For those of us who include this book in our spiritual learning, we often say we like chapter 3 of Daniel because of the boldness of Hananiah, Mishael, and Azariah (also called Shadrach, Meshach, and Abednego, the slave names given to them by their captors), who were willing to say no to the king even if it meant being thrown into literal fire. If we're honest, I think there's another reason. We like Daniel 3 because the three men emerge from the flames without even the stench of smoke on them.

Sometimes life is like that, so I couldn't write about faith without talking about these three furnace dwellers. The three guys in Daniel 3 believed God could do anything, and sometimes I share that certainty. But what about the times when the answer to cries for rescue is no? What happens when the trial is ongoing, the medical condition chronic, and the pain without resolution? Are we willing to radically accept life in the furnace?

I first considered these questions when I was diagnosed with two incurable autoimmune disorders after the birth of our first child. My health has become more complex over the years, and most of my kids have one or more diagnoses, so these questions still echo daily.

Shadrach, Meshach, and Abednego answered and said to the king, "O Nebuchadnezzar, we have no need to answer you in this matter. If this be so, our God whom we serve is able to deliver us from the burning fiery furnace, and he will deliver us out of your hand, O king. But if not, be it known to you, O king, that we will not serve your gods or worship the golden image that you have set up." (Dan. 3:16–18 ESV)

We live in a world in which we're called to bow down to the idol of comfort, as if our ultimate aim in life is ease. When disability or chronic illness enters that world, we can't heed the call anymore to fall down and worship something we were never meant to adore, no matter the consequence. Those of us who believe miraculous healing or medical breakthroughs can happen also know that's not always the outcome from our figurative furnaces.

Then Nebuchadnezzar was filled with fury, and the expression of his face was changed against Shadrach, Meshach, and Abednego. He ordered the furnace heated seven times more than it was usually heated. And he ordered some of the mighty men of his army to bind Shadrach, Meshach, and Abednego, and to cast them into the burning fiery furnace. Then these men were bound in their cloaks, their tunics, their hats, and their other garments, and they were thrown into the burning fiery furnace. Because the king's order was urgent and the furnace overheated, the flame of the fire killed those men who took up Shadrach, Meshach, and Abednego. And these three men, Shadrach,

Meshach, and Abednego, fell bound into the burning fiery
furnace. (Dan. 3:19–23 esv)

We crave the cure. We idolize normalcy. We yearn for an
exit from our seven-times-as-hot furnaces. We watch others be
burned by this world's harshness and hope we will be spared.
Survivors of car accidents or terrorist attacks in which others
died often say in interviews, "God must have been watching out
for me." What does that even mean? That theology sure makes
God out to be an indiscriminate asshole who plays eeny meeny
miny moe with our lives.

Then King Nebuchadnezzar was astonished and rose up in haste.
He declared to his counselors, "Did we not cast three men bound
into the fire?" They answered and said to the king, "True, O king."
He answered and said, "But I see four men unbound, walking in
the midst of the fire, and they are not hurt; and the appearance of
the fourth is like a son of the gods." (Dan. 3:24–25 esv)

I wonder if, as they met the one scholars believe to be the
preincarnate Christ, the three were content in the furnace then.
I wonder if they wanted to stay when Nebuchadnezzar called
them out. I wonder if they had doubts, or if their faith was as
deep in the furnace as it had been before.

Then Nebuchadnezzar came near to the door of the burning
fiery furnace; he declared, "Shadrach, Meshach, and Abednego,

servants of the Most High God, come out, and come here!"
Then Shadrach, Meshach, and Abednego came out from the
fire. And the satraps, the prefects, the governors, and the king's
counselors gathered together and saw that the fire had not had
any power over the bodies of those men. The hair of their heads
was not singed, their cloaks were not harmed, and no smell of
fire had come upon them. (Dan. 3:26–27 esv)

I'd love to say my hair is never singed, my countenance
never harmed, and the stench of the idol I want never upon
me. I'd be lying, though. I've never tried a cigarette, but I smell
like smoke plenty.

I've lived in the furnace. In some ways, I'm still there. Maybe
you're living there right now. Maybe you've made it through the
worst and come out on the other side—smelling of smoke or
not—but still find yourself captive to realities you wouldn't have
chosen. Maybe this isn't the life you dreamed of in the magazine.

Maybe it was never supposed to be.

Maybe the beauty of the furnace is in how it delivers us from
the cheap goods we might have chosen otherwise. Maybe the
purpose is that we rise up with Nebuchadnezzar in worship.
Maybe this is an opportunity to choose conviction over comfort.
Maybe this is one of those "I don't know" moments.

Nebuchadnezzar answered and said, "Blessed be the God of
Shadrach, Meshach, and Abednego, who has sent his angel and
delivered his servants, who trusted in him, and set aside the

king's command, and yielded up their bodies rather than serve and worship any god except their own God." (Dan. 3:28 ESV)

Maybe, just maybe, all of us—no matter what religion we follow, if any—can learn from this story. Maybe in our time in extreme heat, our faith holds as unwavering, or maybe not. Maybe, like in some chemical reactions, the heat changes us. Maybe we prefer cooler weather, but maybe some of what we love about ourselves and others only emerges in the fire.

Maybe furnace living isn't always a bad thing.

CHAPTER 7

HARD TRUST

hey you

yes, you

the one whose smile doesn't reach your eyes

the one whose scars tell a story you're not ready to share

the one who believes you're always too much and never enough

you

are

beautiful

you can

do

this

you are

doing

this

keep doing the next thing

it will not

be

this hard forever

I promise

was eighteen when Lee and I met. My friend Katherine saw him first and thought he was cute, so by the college freshman girl code, she had first dibs. He was certainly pleasing to the eye, and when he laughed, he was all in. A beautifully large smile, a white boy fro similar to Justin Timberlake's hair when he first got popular, and a demonstrative respect for others all made me take notice. But I didn't consider doing anything. He was Katherine's, after all. I only had one semester of college under my belt, at a school six hundred miles from my family and everyone else I knew, and I wasn't going to jeopardize a budding friendship over a boy, no matter how kind he seemed.

I kept scheming to get them together. I would invite her to sit with us if he sat near me. When he asked me to go shopping with him in the French Quarter to find masks for the masquerade ball later that week, part of the college conference we were attending in New Orleans, I asked Katherine to come along.

I thought I was helping Katherine by connecting her to Lee again and again. Lee thought maybe I didn't trust him enough to be alone with him, so he didn't push back because he didn't want to make me uncomfortable. Katherine thought the most clearly of all of us. She realized Lee was into me and not her. So when we were supposed to all meet at a McDonald's a block away from our hotel, she didn't show up. This was before cell phones were super common, with limited plans even if you did have one, so I tried to call her from the phone in the restaurant, thankful they allowed it because I didn't have any change for the pay phone outside. (If you're younger than me, yes, we did use pay phones once upon a time. Also, my first cell phone was nearly the size of a brick. If you can find old episodes of *Saved by the Bell*, take note of Zack Morris's phone. Yep, that's about right.)

I still just thought we were two friends shopping. We laughed. We stopped for a snack. We were obvious tourists. Given my history of being hurt by men, I would have closed myself off more if I had known it was a date. I didn't realize it, though, not until we were walking back to the hotel. He put his arm around me, and I knew. I also was surprised to find that I felt comfortable tucked against him. I didn't want to leave.

So I didn't. I became more comfortable than I knew I could be, able to trust him like I've never trusted any other man. Home for me was with Lee, no matter where we were. And it's been his love that healed me enough to keep living life, now that he's dead.

The conference spanned over New Year's. I'm generally pretty opposed to yearly resolutions because so many are set up to fail and because it feels like too much pressure. But that night, as the year turned to 2001, I made one single resolution with Lee, that we would try to make it work once we were back at school. Then we went back to college for the spring semester and tried that plan. He was in the engineering program at North Carolina State, while I was in the communications program at University of North Carolina, but the schools are only thirty minutes apart. It worked. Our relationship, not without problems, grew and unfolded into the greatest adventure of my life.

But I was terrified. I considered dumping him around the three-month mark because we were starting to know each other well enough for vulnerability, and I was staunchly opposed to that idea then. My friends Sanja and Lara laughed at me when I told them what I was thinking over pizza at The Loop. "Um, yeah, I totally see that, Shannon," Lara said. "He's nice, he treats you like a princess, all of your friends like him, and you are more yourself with him than we've ever seen you. Of course it's time to end it."

Then Lara paused and said, "Do you love him?" I hadn't told anyone yet, but I did. That's what scared me the most. Love is intensely vulnerable. At that stage in my life, vulnerability felt like kryptonite. I broke eye contact with my girlfriends and whispered, "Yes. Yes, I do."

I was scared of loss or abuse or trust, but I wasn't afraid of Lee. As he helped nurse me back to health that semester (I had become seriously ill just a couple of weeks into new classes), he was gentle and tender. He kept showing up. He kept being steady. He kept caring more than any man or boy ever had before.

I never planned for love. I was going to have a job. I was going to do great things. I was going to start a nonprofit. I was going to be independent. I had read the stats that say abuse survivors are more likely than others to be revictimized or to be abusive, and I didn't want either option. I was going to be single to stay safe and keep others safe. I'd talk about weddings or boys or having kids with other girls, but I never meant it, not really.

But then Lee showed up. Just a month into that new year, I

caught the worst case of mono our student health clinic had ever seen. My adviser recommended I leave for the semester, but I didn't want to go back to my childhood home in Florida. I was determined to push through.

Lee couldn't handle mono along with his much heavier course load and much more demanding professors that semester, so we stopped any kissing and hoped he would stay healthy. He did. We had only known each other a matter of weeks, but he showed up for me again and again. He knew I was sick. He knew I'd probably fall asleep as soon as we started a movie, but he let me sleep in his arms while he watched. I'd wake up, shocked that I had felt safe enough to fall asleep yet totally comfortable where I was. My parents' house back in Florida wasn't home anymore, and never really had been, but I finally found home with Lee.

On our first February 14th together, Lee wanted to celebrate Valentine's Day, but he knew I was too sick to go out. He brought a picnic to my dorm room, complete with battery-operated candles so the meal could be by candlelight. (Actual candles weren't allowed, at least not lit, in the dorm. Lee was always a rule follower.) He knew I couldn't swallow much because I had strep throat on top of mono at that point, so he brought subs with soft bread, Gatorade, and chocolate cake. He also brought a teddy bear holding a heart and a bag of Hershey kisses so "I can still give you kisses this way."

I know our story is sappy and sweet, maybe too much so if you're not in a similar relationship right now. But all the pain before led up to these moments for me. Through Lee, God began to heal the bruises and wounds on my heart in a way I didn't know was possible. Romantic love was for other people, not me, I thought before I met Lee. Then we met, and I've never been the same.

————

I thought I'd be writing this book with pain in my past more than in the present. I thought I could trust that love could last, that a happily-ever-after was possible. And it was.

For a while.

My grief was international news because Lee was young and healthy, and who the heck gets killed by a forceful wave on vacation? Our family size and composition, as well as my semi-famous-ish status as a writer and speaker, all factored in as well. I'm not sure I'll ever be able to articulate all the ways that having everyone know your tragic pain is weird and uncomfortable and vulnerable and helpful ("helpful" because of the generosity of friends and strangers who contributed to a GoFundMe campaign set up for us, and also because it's been nice not to wonder if someone knows the news or not—everyone knows).

Lee and I weren't just Instagram-filtered happy. We *were* happy. We were never one of those couples who existed parallel to each other: no, we were always so intertwined that it's hard to tell where one of us ended and the other began. And yet, here we are.

The story of Lee showing up for me on Valentine's Day when I was so sick is a classic Lee story. He showed up in whatever way anyone needed. Maybe it sounds cheesy, but I like to think he's still showing up, in the ways we have been loved so well by others since he died. Together, Lee and I stepped out in faith into so many hard and complex situations, trusting that we didn't need to have it all figured out just yet, but that our people and our God would sustain us. I've ventured into this new and unwanted reality with that same sort of faith.

I think sometimes hope and trust and faith are woven into one. I don't know how I'm going to raise our six amazing kids as a single mom. But I can't do the next thing without a reckless sort of belief—maybe a form of trust or faith or hope—that it's possible.

C. S. Lewis once wrote that death is an amputation, and I told everyone when I spoke at Lee's funeral that it sure felt that way. It still does. I feel like we are missing a part of ourselves. Lee and I had a joke between us, based on the Bible verse about how marriage is two becoming one flesh. We'd be talking to someone, and if they asked something of us and I said, "Sure, we can do that!" then after they walked away, he might whisper, "You meant that as the one-flesh 'we,' right?" And I would reply, "Oh, yeah. I definitely meant you would do it. One flesh, right?" But now I'm the one flesh, without him.

I don't think C. S. Lewis was right, though. His analogy is based in the ableism that says amputation lessens a person, but I know all of us who were touched by Lee are made better and fuller, our hearts made even more whole, by having him in our lives. I trust that will grow and not diminish as the calendar pages turn.

The night I told the kids, one of them pointed to his chest and asked me, "Why does this place right here hurt so badly?" I told him, "It's because you love Daddy big and he loved you big. We have big hurt right now because we had big love." And that's how it's been—we're always changing and growing, even having memories turn a bit blue like in *Inside Out* when Sadness touches them.

Even if I had known where our love story would end, I wouldn't have changed a thing. I know that having known and loved Lee and having been known and loved by him changed me. He made me more of the person that I believe, and he believed, God created me to be. He often told the kids, "Be good humans," and I'm a better human because of him.

Before the funeral, another of the kids remarked, "Dad said once he wanted people to wear bright colors to his funeral and have it be a celebration . . . but I don't think he knew he would die so young." I agreed. I didn't feel comfortable the day we buried him, and I dodged reporters outside the service. He was always bright, though, so I chose a casket in a bright color and had the vault for it painted bright red with an NC State logo on it, which shows how much I love him because—remember—I'm a Carolina girl.

During the initial rush of people showing up for us after he died, one of our youngest ones offered a greeting to some of those visitors. "Hello. This is our house. In this family, we always have big feelings, but especially today. You can cry or you can laugh or you can do whatever you need to do. Whatever you feel is okay."

And it's true. And I trust that what was true will continue to be true as time goes on. It might not, just like Lee didn't come back from the beach as I trusted he would that day. But living without some trust, even a precarious one, feels too untethered from hope for me right now.

I think trust is summed up in Anna's and Elsa's big songs in *Frozen II*. Anna sings of doing the next right thing, trusting that step-by-step she'll figure it out. Elsa sings about venturing into the unknown, trusting herself when everything else is uncertain. As a young widow, I'm doing a little of each, every day.

———

I wasn't certain about much when I graduated college in three years, pushing to do so because I wasn't confident my parents would keep paying the remainder of tuition left after my scholarships. I already bottomed out my savings the one semester they didn't pay, and I almost had to withdraw from classes. I couldn't keep that up. Upon graduation, I moved to Texas to teach special education writing on the Mexican border as part of Teach for America.

Had I ever been to Rio Grande City? No.

Did I know anyone there? Not yet.

The day I arrived, did anyone know I was turning twenty-one the next day? Nope.

But it was my unknown, as Lee finished his engineering degree. Whenever I've charged into uncertainty, having made a move much like this one when I went to college, arriving in Chapel Hill without knowing anyone, church was my constant. I felt like I could trust the ground beneath me if I found myself in the rhythms of a church community again.

For me, church was always sanctuary. Church had brought pain sometimes too, but having grown up in an abusive family, love and pain were tied up in each other in my mind. So upon moving to Texas, finding a new church was at the top of my to-do list. Because I felt most comfortable worshipping in my native language while most of the faith communities in town were led in Spanish, my options were slim. I tried the Catholic church in town, knowing the rhythms of worship would feel similar to my Lutheran upbringing. I also knew most of my students who attended church would be at Mass there. After three Sundays of visiting with not one single person saying hello to me, I began to look elsewhere.

I drove from Rio Grande City, my new place of residence, to McAllen to check out a Lutheran church there. I got lost and never found the place. I stopped for tacos instead, knowing I couldn't go wrong there.

Then I tried one of the two Methodist churches in town. I liked it there. I found friends there, some of them lifelong. But after a handful of Sundays, I felt uneasy that the pastor and most of the congregation were white while we lived in a town that was at least 90 percent Hispanic. I would later learn that years prior, there had only been one Methodist church in Rio, and it split into two over disagreement about what language to use. I had found the English-speaking one, while most of the Hispanic members had stayed at the Spanish-speaking church. Even without knowing the history, I decided it was time to go.

Cue a pivotal conversation with my students' guidance counselor, Annabel, the same woman who challenged me to figure out why I was drinking if I wanted to stay sober. I stopped by her office to ask a question during my planning period. In the course of our conversation, I let her know that I was looking for a church. She was enthusiastic as she invited me to the Southern Baptist church she was attending.

Southern Baptist? I thought. *Well, I guess I can try it.* I never really knew why, but my parents had always said "Southern Baptist" like it was a word that even cable television might censor. I wasn't so sure about going there, but I had no options. I didn't know my heart would become joined to this church forever. I just didn't know where else I could go.

I showed up, hypervigilant in case their theology was whack. All I found were strangers who sought me out and spoke to me like I was a friend. The first to do so was Lori, the organist. She invited me to her home that week for a study using both the Bible and Rick Warren's *The Purpose Driven Life*, the hot book at the time in evangelical circles. Genuine and authentic, she treated me like I belonged there. And so I did.

After a few months, I opened up to her about my childhood abuse. She was a lawyer with experience in family law, so she knew what to ask. "Does Lee hurt you?" she softly inquired. "I'm only asking because it's not uncommon for childhood abuse survivors to be revictimized as adults." My eyes pooled with tears that she probably suspected to be affirmation. They weren't. My eyes were watery because I felt known and cared for. Her empathy and concern landed like an embrace for little childhood Shannon, who didn't know much about those things.

"I totally know what you mean. I've read the research too. I'm glad you asked because it's a question worth asking," I replied. "No. He doesn't hurt me. He never has. He's gentle and kind. And I don't abuse him either, if that's your next question."

She smiled, a relieved half smile that revealed some sadness too. Maybe she was sad for what had happened to me. Maybe she was sad for needing to ask the question at all. "I'm so glad," she said. "Look at you. You're breaking the cycle. The abuse ends with you."

It has. And her question was a version of "Do you trust him?" Well, actually the inverse: "Does he love you?" Please, if you take nothing else away from this book, let it be these two points. First, men who love you don't abuse you. That's not real love. Second, you have to ask the hard questions if we belong to each other. You have to be willing to possibly offend someone, possibly break the trust you once had, by asking if they are safe with their partner. Domestic violence is far too common, and one way we can do something about it is to be willing to ask the questions that require courage.

A couple of years ago, a stranger did this on my behalf. We were both visiting a mutual friend, Dianne, at the hospital while her son was undergoing major surgery. Knowing Dianne's friend was with her, I headed down the hall for the bathroom.

"Is she safe at home?" Dianne's friend asked in a hushed voice as I walked away. I was, and I am, but her concern was well placed. The weekend before I had lost my balance while misjudging the distance between my body and a piece of furniture in a spectacularly graceless moment, slamming my arm hard against solid wood. Two days before, my dog had jerked her paw against my chest, leaving a slight purple mark there. One day before, my son—excited about a video game—pointed at the screen in my lap, scratching his nail against my cheek. Without a doubt, I was wearing plenty of evidence on my skin that I might not be safe.

I don't know her. I probably won't see her again. But? She cared enough for me to ask a mutual friend the hard and awkward question, "Is she safe at home?"

I was, thankfully, and I still am. But other women and children (and men too) aren't safe behind closed doors. Like Lori's question about my well-being, she was checking on a prerequisite for love: safety. In Maslow's hierarchy of needs, each step up requires that the previous step be secure. Before you get to love and belonging, the third level, your safety and physiological needs must be met. They're necessary. You can't opt out of them and try to pole-vault to another level.

I was dressed nicely. I was sporting a new haircut. My accessories were on point. If my husband were present, she would have seen a clean-shaven engineer who doesn't say much unless what he says is better than silence. So many of us assume this picture wouldn't be one of domestic violence. Yet a tweet from Dr. Diane Langberg comes to mind: "[Abusers] can appear to be good friends, loyal employees, or responsible citizens. There are often no telltale signs in an abuser's public behavior."[8]

No one suspected what happened behind closed doors when I was a child. Years later, when I was pregnant with our first child, a fellow youth group volunteer was caught sexually abusing boys at our church. I hadn't suspected anything then. A few years back, an old high school acquaintance was convicted of raping a middle school boy she was tutoring. I thought it must be wrong at first. *Not Ethel!* I thought. But the facts were clear and she confessed, as the explicit text messages between her and the victim were undeniable.

Abuse happens. Your friend might not say anything, but her injuries might speak for her. Be willing to engage in further conversation when they do. If you're wrong—like that well-intentioned friend of a friend was—there's no harm done. But if you're right, you might just open a needed door for healing and safety. If you're right, your one question might be the beginning of her rescue.

When I blogged about this incident, my friend Amy left a comment based on her own life experiences:

> I would add that sometimes a woman tells others what she wishes were true—that she is safe—when she actually is not. I had friends gently but persistently ask multiple times, and when it turned out I was not indeed safe, those women were there to help, no judgment, no "told you so," just immediate help. It's better to ask and be wrong, multiple times even, than to not say anything at all. Ask. And keep asking.

Let's all be brave enough to ask the hard questions when our gut senses something is off. Checking in with your friends about their love and their safety is part of the deal of friendship. "Do you love him?" and "Are you safe?" both require vulnerability to ask and, in greater measure, to answer honestly. But that vulnerability is worth it. It might be weird, sure. But being human always is.

PART IV

TAKING CARE OF YOURSELF IS BRAVE

CHAPTER 8

OUR DESIRES MATTER

I tried
to love my neighbor as myself
doing and
loving and
sacrificing and
providing and
holding space and
giving time and
offering all of myself
pouring out of a dry cistern
to meet their needs
like good girls
are supposed to
nobody taught me that
to love my neighbor as myself
I needed to love me
first

What do you want to do?"

The question seemed simple enough. I looked at my hands, then the floor, then the plate with a child's drawing mounted on the wall. I didn't know the answer. I didn't even know the question. I had never recognized it as something worth considering.

I'm a wife (or, at least, I was at the time this happened). I'm the mom of six elementary school children. I'm a disability inclusion ministry leader. I'm a PTA member. I have Volunteer of the Year awards on my bookshelf.

I don't share all of that to boost my résumé for you, reader. Well, okay, maybe I do like the image that list projects of me, but that's not my only purpose here. I share those roles because they all have something in common: they focus on the wants or needs of others. That's my happy place.

My therapist, Heidi, waited while I looked at the spines of books on her shelves and watched leaves fall from the trees just outside her window. I'm usually good at bullshitting answers, but I couldn't do it this time. Rather than answering the question the way I thought I should, I responded with bare honesty.

"Um, this might sound silly, but that question might as well be in a foreign language. I don't know how to process it. I don't remember the last time anyone asked me what I wanted."

She gave that knowing smile, the one I'm sure must be part of therapist training. I might not know my wants, but I know therapy. Everyone in our family goes to regular counseling. That's just a normal facet of life in a multiracial family in which we're all healing from trauma and coping with chronic health conditions. Heidi might have a couple of decades of experience in her field, but I'm practically a professional at sitting in the client's seat at this point.

My answer wasn't silly, she assured me. She was right. Many of us, especially women, lose ourselves in caring for others. I'm a personality test junkie, and one tidbit about my favorite one has stuck with me. Women often mistype themselves on the enneagram as twos, the number associated with being helpers. Sure, some of us are twos, but in many cases cultural norms drive women to select the answers that point to two, even if their personality is geared toward another number.

(As for me, I'm a six. Loyalty and safety are two central guideposts for me, which makes sense given my life story.)

One Bible story came to mind as I thought about the question. Once upon a time, Mary and Martha were sisters, and Jesus came for a visit. Martha busied herself with the food and hostess responsibilities. I always saw her as the this-is-what-you-should-be character, despite how the story ends. Mary sat at the feet of Jesus, eager for every word of his teaching to lodge deep into her bones. Jesus declared Mary to have made the better choice, but as I look around many churches, I wonder if we're teaching something different. Women aren't encouraged to be the learners, the seminary students, or the scholars of Christianity. We're expected to teach Sunday school—but, in many churches, only to children or other women—and cook for potlucks and maybe sing in the choir or as a backup to the male worship leader. Jesus says we're supposed to be like Mary, but churches across America offer Martha's role as the only one we're allowed to fill or even desire. Being both a nerdy researcher and a terrible hostess, I've always been more of a Mary in any story, but I've long felt like a failure because I don't measure up to Martha.

What did I want? The context for Heidi's question was an upcoming trip to drive a couple of hours to meet my mom and sister for coffee. I wrote in my journal earlier that week, "I wish I could get out of this, but I know I'll go anyway." I said something similar in our session, trying to help her understand that it didn't really matter what I wanted. The family expectation was for me to be there. I'm the youngest child, and I didn't grow up with choices.

"What would happen if you said no?" I didn't roll my eyes at her because I'd only been seeing her a month at this point. I didn't want to appear rude, but an inward eye roll was certainly happening. She didn't get it. In my family, saying no wasn't allowed.

Well, I ended up saying no. And? The world didn't shatter. I didn't break. My mom and sister didn't even yell at me, in part because I backed out via text instead of giving them the chance to guilt me into coming. (In some families, the saying goes, "Home is where the heart is." In ours, home was always where the shame was.) I named what I wanted, I did what I wanted, and no one died as a result.

This moment was pivotal for me. A few months later, I even corrected my barista when I got the wrong drink by mistake. If you're confused by why that's a big deal at all, I'm a little jealous.

I had tried so hard to play small that I would do anything to avoid inconveniencing someone else, even accept an overpriced latte I hadn't ordered while someone else got mine.

Sometimes, unlike that date with my mom or my beverage of choice at the neighborhood Starbucks, getting what we want isn't wise or healthy or even possible. This is important to evaluate. I'm not advocating a thoughtless throwing to the wind of all caution or reason. But even when our wants aren't what's best, we can connect to ourselves enough to know what we truly desire and make informed decisions to pursue that or not.

———

What do I want right now? I want July 19, 2019, to be untrue. I want for none of this to be real. I want for my husband to be alive.

This time, I can't get what I want. I can't get a different outcome to the evening my husband was playing in the ocean with three of our kids one moment and then barely clinging to life with a broken neck the next.

So many people showed up for us immediately and continue to do so. I'm grateful, deeply grateful, for never once feeling like I'm alone in any of this. We're making it, and we'll keep making it.

But I would exchange every bit of kindness for more time with Lee.

I've expressed that in multiple ways on social media, unaware at first that my public grieving was remarkable to anyone. I just shared. Sharing myself online has always been comfortable to me, in part because I wasn't allowed to share much of my true self—publicly or privately—as a child.

Messages and notes kept coming from other grievers who also wanted to be honest about their emotions but didn't feel like they could. They didn't feel understood. Most had tried, had been shut down, and then chose to internalize their desires to avoid disconnection. Keeping everything inside didn't provide connection either, though.

Communicating our desires isn't meant to make them true or speak them into existence. I believe the part of the Genesis creation narrative in which God speaks the world into being. God says it, and it happens. Some people think God is a genie who will provide whatever we speak into existence in faith, but the concept of naming your request to God so that you can claim it—as if God is bound to some agreement to provide what you want when you want it—doesn't line up with what's in the Bible. We say we're created in God's image, but we act like God should be created in our image, agreeing with us and wanting exactly what we want and condemning those we condemn.

If naming the desire and claiming it as God's will were possible, my husband would be alive. He didn't die because of my lack of faith or desire, though. He died because of lack of oxygen to his brain. I saw the scans—the swelling beyond anything recoverable, the uniform color with little difference between white and gray matter, the damage that explained why he wasn't responsive. I could have named and claimed what I wanted every moment of the twenty-two hours I spent by his side in the ICU, but I still would have left without him to give the terrible news to our children.

I did name my wants, though. Our desires do matter. Since he died, I've often said to friends, "I just want him back." They know and I know that my want isn't something to fix or bring to fruition. He's at Raleigh's Historic Oakwood Cemetery, not Stephen King's *Pet Sematary*, after all. But saying what I want is important. My wanting words are not meant to conjure Lee's spirit, to beg someone else to right the wrong, or to deny reality. No, sometimes naming our desires is important because telling the truth about what we want helps us connect better with ourselves and each other.

Sometimes recognizing the importance of a desire isn't about making it happen. Sometimes it's simply wrapping words around a yearning so others can understand what is so strong within us that it almost feels tangible. It is important for me to say that I want Lee back, even knowing it's not going to happen.

———

In 2012, I named a want and asked for help. Lee and I were preparing to adopt a baby girl with complex medical needs from Taiwan. Zoe is now the light of our family and community, but we hadn't met her yet then. We had pictures, her name, and a pile of paperwork to be completed. During the process that would make me a mom for the third time, I craved something I hadn't had for years.

What did I want? Alcohol, that's what. I was almost eight years sober when we were adopting Zoe. My desire for alcohol surprised me.

It was the worst possible time to consider taking another drink. I hadn't disclosed to our social worker that I had any substance abuse history. I didn't mean to deceive her. I had just been pretending for so long that I thought I was telling the truth.

I had begun to question if alcohol was ever really a problem for me anyway. When I was young, my mom's verbal abuse often included accusations of being dramatic whenever I told the truth. Maybe she was right, I wondered, hearing her voice to me in childhood as my inner critic in adulthood. Maybe what I considered alcohol abuse was never that bad. (Spoiler alert: It was.) Maybe I had imagined it all, I reasoned. Yet I knew the ferocity with which I wanted a drink wasn't normal.

There I was, with everything going wonderfully my way, with miracles and promise abounding around every corner. Nothing in my life had ever been this good. Yet all I wanted was to drown in tequila.

I didn't know what to think other than, *Wait, what?* No one knew about my substance abuse history except for my husband. We were already in the process of turning our lives upside down via adoption and selling a house and buying a house and preparing our oldest child for kindergarten. Back then, I felt like I had to protect those I loved the most from any darkness in me.

Wanting to drink felt like the lights had gone out, just for me, while everyone else could still bask in the light. I didn't want to turn off the lights for Lee too. I didn't know how to find the light switch, though, and then I remembered I knew someone who might: Melinda.

While Melinda and I would become best friends, we were only acquaintances then. We had been in a couple of Bible studies together. We had mutual friends galore. We weren't really friends yet, but I could remember the first night I met her. It was three years before we adopted Zoe, back when I was five years sober and the mother of a newborn. I was sitting on an ottoman, my chest uncomfortable. My two-month-old son was nursing regularly, and this was my first evening away from him. I was the youngest woman in the room by at least a decade. I knew the other women would probably understand, but as I sat there, I hoped and prayed my swollen breasts wouldn't leak through my shirt.

Because a few of us, myself included, were new, we had been asked to introduce ourselves. Because we were a group of conservative Christian ladies in the South, we couldn't just do that in a straightforward way. No, an icebreaker was necessary. We paired up and shared our names with our partners, as well as one unique fact and the dream job we'd love to have. Then we each took turns introducing our partners. Starting at the couch to my left, we looped around to the armchair and then to those sitting on the floor. I don't remember my answers, but I do remember Melinda's. She sat on a cushion next to the fireplace, and I had already noticed her laugh because it seemed more life-giving than anyone else's in the room. Her partner shared her name, along with the fact that Melinda had been valedictorian of her high school class here in Raleigh. (Clearly, she and I both have the knack for résumé sharing when we first meet someone, just like I did at the start of this chapter.) But it was her dream job that piqued my interest, with the words barely audible as we were all still laughing at the rich ridiculousness of a grown woman offering her high school stats in an icebreaker. Her partner shared that if Melinda could have any job, she would want to be an addiction and substance abuse counselor. Our host, Norma, said, "Wait, wasn't that what you used to do?" and Melinda replied, "Yes, but I loved it. I hope to return to it one day."

"She would be safe," I immediately thought. I have this habit of classifying people as unsafe (most people) or safe (a rare few). I can't remember a time I didn't do it. In a room of mostly Southern Baptist women, Melinda dared to not only bring up drugs and alcohol but do so in a way that offered no condescension. She had loved the work, simple as that. As a woman who hid her past substance abuse like a dirty secret, I felt buoyed by Melinda's nonchalance.

I didn't say anything to her that night. I had moved to Raleigh four summers before from South Texas, where my friends saw me through getting sober. When I moved to North Carolina, I wanted to be allowed to volunteer with the high school girls at church. I didn't know if they would let me if they knew I had only been sober for one year.

My solution was to not tell them at all. Then I kept not telling anyone. I didn't mean to keep it a secret from everyone but
my husband, but that's what happened. After keeping my silence
for a while, I wasn't sure how to bring it up. Plus every friend I
had made by that summer shared the common story of having
grown up in safe Christian homes, at least as they each described
their upbringings. I wanted the same for myself, so I pretended.

Until I met Melinda, I hadn't found anyone who I thought
might be able to handle my story. I didn't speak with her that
night. I'm not sure we even talked for a few more weeks. But I
knew once I was ready, she might be a possibility.

So when that nursing baby boy was three years older and we
were adding to our family via adoption, I messaged Melinda online. She still didn't know my secret. We had exchanged several
messages before this one, many diving well below surface level,
but this one brought a new level of intimacy. This was my cry
for help, albeit framed as being just fine because that's what I
always claimed to be. Instead of trying to recite it from memory,
I'm pulling up my old messages as I write this, having to go back
years to find any from Melinda. As I search, her name is making
me blink back tears.

Here are my words, written with uncertainty and a side of
hope in the spring of 2012:

Could we do dinner or coffee some evening soon? I know
there's a lot of end-of-year stuff going on, but I've driven
past your neighborhood a half-dozen times in the past

week or two and thought each time, "I would LOVE to have some sweet time with Melinda!"

And to be completely transparent, this is a little bit about wanting to get together with a friend who understands substance abuse. I'm not in an emergency situation, but I know myself well enough to know I'm not in a good place and I need to let other people know what I'm struggling with right now.

I know I've mentioned in Bible study that I grew up in an alcoholic home and that I drank a lot at times, but I don't think I've shared about my own battles with alcohol. (Or have I?) I've been sober for a little over eight years, and I have only recently started sharing much about that with friends here. I didn't share that with people when I arrived in Raleigh, even with close friends, because my sobriety was still new when Lee and I got married and I moved up here and I was concerned then that I would be judged for it or identified by it. Then it became a nonissue—I wasn't desiring alcohol or drunkenness, and it rarely crossed my mind, except when I would pass by the wine section in a grocery store. I got to the point at which I could have it in our home for cooking (I love the taste of pork cooked in white wine!) without any temptation, which was big for me.

The first year of sobriety was rough, but I haven't missed alcohol in the past seven years. Until now. With all the changes going on, those old desires have reemerged and caught me off guard. I'll think, "Wow, what I wouldn't give for a drink right now," and then think, "Wait, what? I don't want to be back there, and I've not had that thought for years."

Her reply began, "I'm honored that you shared this with me, and it would be a privilege to get together with you and hear more of your story." My instinct that she was safe was an accurate one, clearly. We got together regularly until I was through that season, and then we got together regularly because we were friends. I knew what she really thought about her sons' girlfriends, and she knew about our next adoption before anyone else. We shared mental health struggles. We each knew which meds the other took and complained together when side effects were unpleasant. I reached out to her because I needed help, but what I wanted was more. I wanted a friend. Furthermore, as someone who had hidden my true self for years, I wanted to learn how to be a friend. She gave me both gifts.

I just wish she had been able to make the same sort of risky ask at the end of March 2015. I wish she could have named or communicated what she wanted in her darkest moment so someone could help her be safe until she wanted life again. I knew she was going through a med shift. I knew she was struggling. We had lunch together in mid-March, and I was concerned. I kept reaching out to her in the coming weeks, and she seemed to be on top of her health.

Her second-to-last text to me was a week after that lunch. She shared that her sleep was messed up and admitted she had "slid rather quickly into a place I hate to go (ughhh)." She canceled a long-planned trip, at the recommendation of her doctor, to focus on her mental health. She said she was embarrassed, "even telling you," she added.

My last text to her said, "No embarrassment, my friend. You chose what's best and healthiest for you, even though it was a hard choice, and I'm proud of you." A few days after that text, she was gone. As some people succumb to diseases like breast cancer, Melinda's fatal illness was depression. I hate suicide, and I miss Melinda every day. I wish her illness hadn't made it impossible for her to see life as something she could keep wanting.

To honor Melinda, I decided I would get serious about prioritizing my health. I didn't know this word then, but self-care was what I had in mind. Some of you tend to side-eye this topic. I see you. You're not alone. I have a dear friend who has blocked all tweets with #selfcare in them because she's so sick of this trend. For many of us, though, self-care is saving our lives.

Melinda cared well for everyone else, always. Would she have had a better chance of surviving if she had prioritized taking care of herself? I don't know. I don't think that question is worth exploring. She tried. I know how hard she tried. I don't blame her one bit for what her illness did to her. But knowing how well she had cared for me, I resolved I would continue that good care in her absence. Then, a few months after she died, I heard the phrase "self-care" for the first time.

I'm not sure how I missed it before then. Now you can't get

far in our culture without hearing about self-care. Earlier in this chapter, I've already identified two of my sources for that: therapy and lattes. For me, self-care often looks like the answer to this chapter's question. What do I want? The answer varies depending on my mood, but some common desires are relaxing in bubble baths, reading from just about any genre, petting our small zoo of animals, rewatching *The West Wing*, taking communion at church each Sunday, lighting aromatic candles, or getting one-on-one time with those I love. This list is mostly superficial, even if you add two basic self-care tasks: eating meals regularly and taking my daily meds. For me, it's most often the small acts—in between more profound forms of self-compassion—that matter the most.

When I met my current therapist and plopped down on her red couch, I was trying out therapy for the first time in more than a decade because something felt out of whack. I couldn't put my finger on it. For me, writing is like breathing; I can't live without doing it. In the fall of 2015, all our kids were in school together for the first time. I had grand plans of finally writing a book, playing with words during the day as they played with learning and friends. But school started, and the writing didn't come. I couldn't write. It wasn't writer's block. This was more like writer's barricade. Never having experienced this before, I was disoriented. I didn't know what was wrong, but I asked myself what Melinda would recommend if she were still alive. I knew the answer immediately, realizing it was time to seek help.

I put it off, though. Good intentions only take you so far. As much as I knew that I needed to talk to a professional, I didn't want to do it. Melinda was only in the grave six months at that point. Then another woman at our church died by suicide, a young mom whom I never knew well but with whom I shared too much in common. I knew what it was like to be suicidal from a particularly dark stretch in my youth, and though I didn't see those desires bubbling to the surface in me again, I remembered the feelings. With Melinda and this young mom, people kept saying, "I can't believe that could happen to someone like her." All I could think was "This just happened again to someone like me." I didn't want to be the third one.

I texted my friend Sam, asking for mental health professionals she'd recommend. She texted back the name of someone she trusted. I emailed that psychologist, found out she didn't take my insurance, and then called the number of another therapist at her suggestion. Heidi called back. I told her more on the phone than I intended, and we set up a time for an intake session.

I canceled that session, citing strep throat. The reality was that while I was on antibiotics for strep, I was almost done with the course of meds. I felt fine. I just didn't feel like exposing my inner world to a stranger. Part of me hoped she would drop me as a client, but she didn't. We rescheduled for the next week. I hate letting people down, so I showed up that time, more out of obligation than a personal desire to be there.

I cussed under my breath as I walked out of that first appointment. I thought we'd talk about the massive transition of adopting several children and going from a family of four to one of eight in fifteen months. My problem, I was sure, was adjustment issues. Our lives were not only full of more people but they were also packed with more appointments, more diagnoses, more racial dynamics, more languages, and more activity. My attitude was like Dr. Brené Brown's when she first stepped into therapy, which she writes about in *The Gifts of Imperfection*:

> Diana, who is a therapist to many therapists, started with the requisite, "So what's going on?" I pulled out the *Do* list and matter-of-factly said, "I need more of the things on this list. Some specific tips and tools would be helpful. Nothing deep. No childhood crap or anything."[9]

That didn't work out so well for Brené with Diana, and it didn't work for me with Heidi either. As Heidi and I talked, my childhood crap leaked out of the airtight story I planned to tell.

As far as childhoods go, mine wasn't great. (Heidi would say that last sentence is an example of my tendency to minimize. She would be right.) I first learned bad words as I was called them, first learned about sex through porn exposure and abuse from male family members, first learned to take care of myself because no one else was doing it, and first started drinking alcohol regularly when I was eleven because I could and because I liked how it made me forget how much I was hurting. By my rationale, I didn't need to talk to Heidi about any of that. I had seen a different therapist when I was in my early twenties. We talked about my early years. Then I figuratively boxed up all that hard truth and tucked it on the highest bookshelf to rest there, unopened and unmoved, forever. Just like I pretended alcohol abuse was no longer an issue to our adoption social worker, I was content pretending my early life was no longer an issue to myself.

Trauma doesn't work that way, though. It demands to be known. I didn't want to own my story, so my story was owning me. Pieces of the story, details I thought I could ignore till kingdom come, trickled out in that intake session. Heidi's eyes reflected a compassion that made me uncomfortable, as she gently said, "I'm so sorry that happened to you."

I didn't think I needed to hear those words. I shrugged when she said them. For the next week, though, those compassionate words echoed in my mind. I knew therapy was going to involve discussing more than recent transitions. I was ready for that when I showed up the next week.

But she didn't go there.

I bet you can guess where she pivoted. Yep, self-care. I hope my face didn't show my skepticism, but I know I thought, *Seriously? I opened up about pain I've hidden for a decade, and now you want to backtrack to talk about buying a candle to light while I'm in the tub?* I didn't get it. I decided to play along, but if I'm honest, I thought that maybe Heidi wasn't too good at this whole counseling gig after all. I stuck it out with her, but mostly because I couldn't bear the idea of opening up to someone else.

She was right, of course. I found myself frustrated at my first self-care attempts. I am a recovering perfectionist. Give me an assignment, and I'm all over it. I achieve. It's what I do. But taking care of myself? Showing self-compassion? Learning to be and not just do? This was all new territory for me, and I wasn't great at it. Heidi must have sensed that because she gently suggested, "And give yourself permission to do it imperfectly."

Now I consider self-care to be a spiritual practice. Some people consider asking yourself, "What do I want?" to be a selfish habit. But the call to love others as you love yourself assumes you love yourself in the first place, right? It can be both/and: both caring for ourselves and caring for others, both identifying what we want and hearing what others want, both putting on our own oxygen mask and helping others secure their own.

———

If you grew up with familial or theological abuse, this concept of listening well to what you want might seem weird. It did for me at first, and it still does more often than I'd like to admit. We come by it naturally.

The message conveyed to an abuse victim is "What you want doesn't matter." Abuse is about control. (I want to highlight that this includes sexual assault. Some people think rape is about sex, but that's a fallacy. Sex crimes are about power over another. All abuse is about power, in one way or another.)

Power bestows privilege, or maybe it's the other way around. Power isn't always bad, of course. When a parent exercises benevolent power with a child, for example, the purpose is provision for the child's wants or needs. Bosses hold the power to hire or fire or set pay and benefits. Spiritual leaders are often presented as the representatives of a higher power, sometimes—as in the Roman Catholic Church until the Second Vatican Council in the 1960s—with the language used by religious leaders differing from the common language of the people, limiting access to spiritual truth linguistically. Historically and today, literacy and literature access also provide both privilege and power, both in religious contexts—as with the Gutenberg Bible allowing greater access to Christian scripture in the 1450s than any prior time—and in professional and educational contexts, which then translate to economic opportunities. Meanwhile, the power of many cultures is also based in language, with cultural disconnect or even erasure resulting from a loss of original language. In patriarchal societies, being assigned male gender at birth can also provide power and privilege. Everywhere I have traveled or lived—the US, Guyana, Ecuador, Uganda, Taiwan, and parts of Europe—offered some degree of power and privilege to me because I'm white.

Power and privilege aren't abuse, though, not by themselves. Through my research of and experience with abuse, I've come to a clear working definition: abuse is the result whenever power and privilege are combined with ignorance of or disregard for the interests, desires, or needs of those lacking power and privilege.

To demonstrate the value of our shared humanity, if what I want matters, then what you want must matter too. Conversely, if what you want matters, then what I want must matter. In the words of Rumi, we're all just walking each other home, and in the words of Glennon Doyle, there's no such thing as other people's children. Abuse is inevitable whenever we equate the power or privilege (or lack thereof) of a person with their worth or intrinsic value or even their degree of humanness.

Because we don't live in a power-neutral society, the potential for abuse is always present. For example, even verbalized consent isn't genuine consent if coercion is present through active pressuring or a more passive power differential. Yes can't mean yes unless no is also an acceptable option without significant consequences.

Yes and no are both important expressions of our wants and desires. If you've experienced abuse, you were painfully taught that your yes and your no weren't relevant or important. That was a lie, but it's a hard one to unlearn. The practice of unlearning the lies of abuse is a daily one for me, so if it is for you too, you're not alone.

———

So, what do you want?

(I meant that as a rhetorical question, but if something comes to mind, please pause to reflect upon or share it. Maybe write it in the margins or text it to a friend. Your desires are important, so if an answer came to mind immediately, please don't ignore it.)

The next time you're struggling with a situation, pause and ask yourself, "What do I want here?" Give yourself permission to consider your own desires instead of automatically catering to everyone else's. If you have the resources and privilege to do so, get yourself to therapy to partner with someone to explore this question more fully, particularly if you have some heavy unlearning to do when it comes to considering yourself or your desires to be valuable.

More than anything, though, here's a lesson I've been learning for myself lately. It holds true for all of us, no matter how it plays out:

You matter, and what you want matters.

Even if that seems like a foreign concept, it is absolutely the truth.

Promise.

CHAPTER 9

OUR FEELINGS ARE GOOD INFORMATION

nothing
is wrong
with your feelings
notice them
welcome them
befriend them
hold space for them all
instead of casting them
and casting them off
as enemies
sometimes
what we do with those feelings
might be wrong or harmful
but those feelings themselves
are not to blame
let your feelings inform choices
but
don't give them permission
don't give them the driver's seat
don't let them carry you away

from your integrity
choose wisely, my friend
with the treasure chest of feelings
you receive
it is a gift

You can't trust your feelings. After all, 'the heart is deceitful above all things, and desperately wicked,' a truth written by the prophet Jeremiah."

Growing up in a patchwork experience of multiple churches and Christian settings, I've heard some variation of that sentence more times than I can count. That version of Jeremiah 17:9 is from one Christian translation (KJV) of the Hebrew Bible, but other versions describe the heart as "beyond cure" (NIV) or "desperately sick" (ESV).

From interpretations of this verse and other passages often cited about the flesh or the heart, I was certain of one thing: everything that made me human also made me bad. When I went to conservative fundamentalist youth groups, what we were taught to think about ourselves on Wednesday nights after the guitars and drums faded away was that we were always inferior, less than, and totally depraved, and God wasn't—simplified to *Tarzan* language: me bad, you bad, Jesus good.

Maybe it might have been less damaging if the Jesus good part was emphasized, like an embrace of words. It wasn't, though. We received the verbal punches of "me bad" and "you bad" ten times for every one verbal hug saying "Jesus good."

That didn't end in high school either. When I was in my late twenties, I attended a pastor's conference in my city. No one invited me. No one would have in those theological circles. I, after all, am a woman. All the speakers were men. All the invited pastors were men. But registration was open, and I've never been much for arbitrary rules. I don't understand theologically conservative male ministry leaders who belittle women's ministry events yet never consider that those same women are marginalized or even excluded from the same educational opportunities the men pursued.

(In their framework, gender is binary. While I don't agree that it is, I've used binary language here because I'm describing the environment as it was. As a cis woman, I raised eyebrows when I entered the room, but I don't think a gender-creative person would have even been allowed through registration. At that time, I didn't realize this privilege, and I don't think I knew nonbinary identity—that is, identifying as neither male nor female or as both—existed.)

Recently, I found my notes from that conference. I remember berating myself that first morning because I forgot a notebook. *How could I be taken seriously as a learner if I didn't even come prepared? Stupid, stupid, stupid.* When I wandered through the expo hall, I met someone at the booth for a largely unknown fundraising platform, and the freebie you got for listening to their spiel was a notebook. On the first page, I wrote:

I did not deserve this book.

I accepted it from the generosity of the Razoo guy.

I do not deserve grace.

I do not deserve a role in ministry.

I do not deserve Lee.

I do not deserve my kids.

I do not deserve my home.

I do not deserve my friends.

I do not deserve the home I came from.

I do not deserve anything.

I deserve hell.

"I deserve hell" wasn't something I picked up as an implication; no, I can think of seven pastors along the way who taught that explicitly, without a single one of them affirming the goodness of God's creation in us, the original blessing ignored as they focused on the original curse.

The grace part I still believe. Grace by definition is unmerited favor. The whole point is that it's undeserved. I don't deserve grace. Neither do you. If we deserved it, it wouldn't be grace anymore, by definition. Grace is God saying, "Yes, this is yours, and I say you deserve it because it's mine to give."

I wish I had a time machine to visit my former self in the moment I wrote that list and let her know she is worthy of so much more than she felt she was then. But I was sure my heart was always and forever deceitful, and I wore a necklace then with the words "Anything good you see in me is Christ," so I don't think

2011 me would have listened, even to another version of me. The beauty of fundamentalism is how clear the rules are.

That's also the danger of it.

——

"Shannon, do you realize you're smiling while you talk about the horrific abuse you survived?"

No, I hadn't, not until Laura pointed it out. (Laura's my backup therapist for when Heidi's unavailable.) I had, however, observed that people are often uncomfortable with tears and un-accustomed to meeting raw pain personified. The only way I knew to tell my story was to plaster on a smile to put the other person at ease. Juxtaposed with stories many would call un-speakable, though, my well-intentioned smile was as creepy as Heath Ledger's smile as the Joker.

In my mind, feelings—and especially expressing them—were perpetually tangled with shame and judgment. To survive childhood trauma, I learned to dissociate, which is basically dis-connecting from your body and emotions. That worked for me for so long that it felt both superior and preferable to feelings, even though I was numb to everything, positive or negative or somewhere in between.

I was so opposed to feeling that even as I began to open up about my abuse, my face never matched the story. I didn't know how to have my insides and outsides match. No, rather than get-ting curious about feelings, I put them on trial right away, with the mean girl in my head serving as both judge and jury. Guilty was always the verdict rendered.

But feelings can't be judged. They need to be explored. Any teaching that God wants us to suppress our emotions is bullshit. I know that's a strong word, but I'm not sorry for it. A more accurate translation of the Apostle Paul's use of "rubbish" in Philippians 3:8 would be "dung" or "shit,"[10] and Malachi 2:1–9, in the original Hebrew, calls empty sacrifices "dung," again, or "bullshit."[11] I stand by my language.

In the Bible, we read imprecatory psalms, many that sound like curses from a book of spells rather than scripture from a life-giving volume of wisdom. They are rich with the full range of feelings. Consider this excerpt from Psalm 69 (NIV):

You know how I am scorned, disgraced and shamed;
    all my enemies are before you. . . .
May their eyes be darkened so they cannot see,
    and their backs be bent forever.
Pour out your wrath on them;
    let your fierce anger overtake them.

Or what about this from Psalm 109 (NIV):

May [my enemy's] days be few;
    may another take his place of leadership.
May his children be fatherless
    and his wife a widow.
May his children be wandering beggars;
    may they be driven from their ruined homes.

May a creditor seize all he has;
    may strangers plunder the fruits of his labor.
May no one extend kindness to him
    or take pity on his fatherless children.

Or take a look at these lines from Psalm 6 (NIV):

I am worn out from my groaning.

All night long I flood my bed with weeping
    and drench my couch with tears.
My eyes grow weak with sorrow;
    they fail because of all my foes.

    The feelings these psalms express aren't polite or nice or pretty. They are real. Some come out as wishes against others, like when someone says, "I'd like to slap that smile off her face," as an expression of how they feel about her. Literally slapping that smile off her face would be wrong in almost all cases, but admitting you feel like doing so? That's human.

    Feelings are amoral. They aren't right. They aren't wrong. They simply are. What we do with our feelings is what can be either okay or not okay. (Going back to the Bible for a moment, I want to point out that Jesus flipped over tables in anger. That tells me that it can be okay to choose a path of acting on feelings, even if it doesn't fit the sweet Southern lady mold I'm told by my culture to embody.)

    The common pushback on this is that feelings aren't always honest. Again, I call bullshit on that. Feelings are deeply honest, but they aren't always objectively true. That's part of why feelings are so damn tricky. But when did we start believing the lie that only truth matters and not also honesty? Being 100 percent in our feelings without ever engaging our intellect is unwise, but so is being 100 percent in our intellect without ever engaging our feelings. I remain curious about both. What's going on inside of me? Why am I convinced of this intellectually? Where are these feelings blooming from, and what are their roots?

And while vulnerability—the act of engaging with our feelings and even exposing them to others who have earned the right to that kind of intimacy—can feel terrifying, learning to feel what we feel is essential to presenting our full selves in any context. We don't have to wear our hearts recklessly on our sleeves at all times, but it is good and healthy when our insides and our outsides aren't in conflict, like my outer smile was while expressing deep inner pain from my past.

———

I'd love for my most used sentence to be "I believe you" or "You matter" or "I love you." I might come close with "Be kind" or "We don't do hurts," both common parenting catchphrases around our house. But, no, I think the sentence I've said the most in my life is "Does this make sense?"

As a public-school teacher, I did checks for understanding with my middle school students to make sure they were learning what I thought I was teaching. Likewise, I did checks for understanding with everyone else. I told myself I was checking my communication skills, making sure my message was clearly understood. But the truth was that I sought outside affirmation for my feelings. I wanted to make sure they made sense. Often, after I had shared my emotions with my therapist, I'd follow with "Does that make sense?"

After hearing me ask a hundred or so times, Heidi said, "Yes, that totally makes sense. But even if it didn't make sense to me, Shannon, it wouldn't matter. It's how you feel. You don't need permission to feel what you're feeling."

Maybe you already knew this. I certainly didn't.

Her words reminded me of those of another wise woman, J. K. Rowling. During an out-of-body experience after Voldemort strikes Harry with a killing curse, Harry is reunited with Dumbledore in a dreamlike state. At one point, Harry asks if the whole scene is in his head. In classic fashion, Dumbledore replies, "Of course it is happening inside your head, Harry, but why on earth should that mean that it is not real?"[12]

Heidi might as well have said, "Of course the feelings are uniquely yours, but why on earth would that mean they don't make sense?"

———

When Lee died, absolutely nothing made sense. There's no normative data about what makes sense to do when your young husband's death makes you a young widow to six young children. Even if there had been, every person's grief is unique.

I sat across from the trauma doctor in the ICU family conference room, sand still covering my shins from when I knelt next to Lee's barely breathing body on the beach. I wasn't ready. I don't think anyone can ever be ready.

The doctor's words felt far away. "Devastating" was a word he repeated several times. He apologized for not having better news for me, and I shrugged it off.

"It's okay," I started to say, but the doctor didn't let me finish.

"No," he said firmly. "No. Nothing about this is okay. It's not okay that you're getting this news today."

In that moment, everything rushed in: the words, the reality, the pain. I still didn't notice the sand on my legs, but I felt everything else. "Hypoxic brain damage," I asked, in a tone too flat to make the questioning intent clear, but the doctor understood. Our youngest child has cerebral palsy, so I know about brain injuries. Hers was different, but I knew hypoxia—lack of oxygen to the brain—was serious.

"Yes. Would you like to see the brain scans?"

I did. Brain scans don't lie. Words aren't always honest, but images don't sugarcoat anything. As soon as I saw the scans, only three hours after the accident, I knew I would be leaving the hospital as a widow.

To confirm what I already knew, I summoned the bravery

to ask, "So we're in the realm of a miracle being the only way he survives, right?"

This doctor, his face both kind and clear, looked me in the eyes. "I've seen miracles," he said, "but never in a case like this, never with damage this devastating."

I looked at the scan, smooth edges where his beautiful brain was swollen against his skull, almost no shade differentiation between white and gray matter. The image looked like it might be on an anatomy test, a brain with key features missing for students to draw and label. But this wasn't a test. This was life.

The scan made sense, but it still doesn't make sense to me that my husband, the best man I ever knew, had that brain inside his skull. I knew that sort of brain would never move a mouth to say "I love you" or innervate arms to wrap around me. We were eighteen and nineteen when we met and began dating. In that ICU room, we were both thirty-seven. But I knew I was the only one of us who would ever turn thirty-eight.

His death didn't make sense. It still doesn't. So it seems fitting that the feelings don't make sense. They aren't supposed to.

Grief is never one-size-fits-all because feelings don't abide by any rules or boundaries. Grief simply is. Feelings simply are. There has never been one right way to feel or grieve, never one universal road map, never a guidebook to follow. How we feel is good information for our relationships, actions, and words, but those feelings rarely make sense.

They aren't meant to.

———

In our house, we talk about big feelings. We did years before Lee died. I wrote this section as a blissfully ignorant wife and mom who never would have imagined the nightmare of July 19, 2019, and I'm leaving the words as they were then, written by a woman and about children who never knew the depth and range of feelings that would come in their near future.

"Are you having big feelings?"

"Mom, I'm having big feelings right now."

"Today at school, Avery had some big feelings."

Instead of unpacking what this means in my words, I'm going to let my kids—currently ages seven, eight, ten, ten, twelve, and twelve—explain it in their words. (Again, these are their descriptions from before their dad died.)

TWELVE-YEAR-OLD GIRL: "Big feelings can be overwhelming, and it's hard to breathe, and I forget all my strategies for self-regulation. Usually I can't explain what I'm feeling in the moment, and that makes the feelings bigger, and it seems impossible to hold them until I'm with someone safe and can share them."

TWELVE-YEAR-OLD GIRL: "Big feelings are those feelings that make you want to yell or scream or cry or shout, even if you can't do that. I get more big feelings when I'm hungry than when I'm not, so sometimes you and Dad give me a snack to help me find my self-control before we can talk about it."

TEN-YEAR-OLD BOY: "Big feelings are so big that they're hard to understand, even if you're having them. They're the ones you get when all your logic goes away and everything fills with feeling."

TEN-YEAR-OLD BOY: "Big feelings are feelings that are too much to deal with alone, without help. Sometimes my big feelings come out in different ways because I'm autistic."

EIGHT-YEAR-OLD GIRL: "I like big feelings when they're happy, but sometimes I feel big mad or big sad or big jealous or big left out or big tired."

SEVEN-YEAR-OLD GIRL: "Everybody has big feelings sometimes. Daniel Tiger taught me about them."

(If your kids don't talk like this, please remember that we talk about big feelings a lot, almost all of us go to therapy, and they have a mom who reads journal articles about psychology and interpersonal communication for fun. In other words, just like a kid living in a Spanish-speaking home usually learns Spanish, my kids live in a feelings-speaking home. It's who we are.)

Do you see what's missing from each of their definitions? Judgment. They get that feelings are normal and neutral. If you feel it, then it makes sense. It's what we do with feelings that matters.

We talk about big feelings in this way because we want to learn together how to notice the feelings as observers. We're often told we need to move through feelings, but I like to think of them as passengers in a car I'm driving. They are there. They are worthy of being noticed. They might even help with navigation, looking at the map while I keep my eyes on the road.

But feelings don't get to drive.

CHAPTER 10

KEEPING OUR HEALTH

i see you
calling need weak
and dependence failure
but you, brave one
you are human
and that is no cosmic mistake
it's time to
retire the cape that
never was meant for you
be bold enough
to admit need
be strong enough
to depend on others
and
above all
be gentle
with your beautiful human heart

Maybe you have postpartum depression?" Lee hesitantly suggested.

I loved my husband for many reasons, but his willingness to ask the hard questions is near the top of the list. I was so tired I didn't argue. That was probably one of the signs to him that I wasn't myself.

Our firstborn was eight months old. I was sick. We didn't know why. My husband knew I needed help. He asked me to see my doctor. I agreed.

And I was terrified. I was only twenty-five years old. I was a brand-new mom. I had only been married two years. I didn't know what was wrong, just that I felt wrong.

Within the next year, we thought I had cancer and then ruled it out. We discovered that my thyroid didn't work anymore because of an autoimmune disorder called Hashimoto's disease. Basically, my overachieving immune system got a little confused, thought my thyroid was a sickness in need of eradication, and shut it down, not knowing that I really needed that little butterfly-shaped organ for metabolism and endocrine function. Then we found out that my superhuman immune system was also attacking the lining of my joints via an illness called rheumatoid arthritis.

Then, a week after finding out I had RA, I peed on a stick and the right number of lines showed up to tell us that our daughter's days of being an only child were numbered. I was still sick. My treatment wasn't figured out. Now new life was growing inside of me, even as other parts of my body short-circuited.

The gift of youth kept me from understanding the gravity

of the situation. Just like when Lee and I took a bus through Mexico without getting the proper visas a few years before this, being young can make us irrationally bold. Sick and pregnant, I wasn't worried. I had survived my childhood. My baby and I would survive this. I was certain, for no good reason.

To survive, I needed high doses of steroids throughout the entire pregnancy. The immunosuppressant qualities of prednisone, combined with my already erratic immune system, led to a serious skin infection of MRSA (Methicillin-resistant Staphylococcus aureus), which is a common and dangerous form of antibiotic-resistant bacteria. I had an immediate in-office surgical procedure, and—on the way home—called Lee to casually let him know that we would need to order pizza when his parents came over the next day because I wouldn't be up for cooking. I added, as an afterthought, that I'd just had some surgery, the wound was left open, and the dressing needed to be changed a few times a day. He knew I was stubbornly independent, but even he was surprised that I didn't try to contact him as I signed the consent form for surgery. I didn't understand until recently that people could genuinely care about me, and I grew up accustomed to life without support. It never would have occurred to me to say anything to anyone because I didn't know anyone would care very much.

A pharmacist, three doctors, and one physician's assistant worked together to find a safe treatment that wouldn't harm me or my baby, the amazing ten-year-old we now call Robbie. I spent the rest of the pregnancy sick or in pain. You know those women who glow when they're with child, whose skin clears up and whose autoimmune disorders go into remission? Good for them. I've never been that sort of woman in my pregnancies. I'm past those days now, but when I was still in the thick of it, I was envious of those women.

I gave birth, with IV steroids pumped into me to help that happen. The long-term course of steroids made my adrenaline system rely on artificial means, and it didn't know how to kick into gear on its own. We held our precious son, and I thought that chapter of pain was drawing to an end. I started on IV medication to treat my rheumatoid arthritis and tweaked my thyroid meds as my body's needs changed through a year of nursing, which I fought with my specialists to be able to do.

(To be clear, I'm not offering subtle judgment of anyone who doesn't breastfeed. I firmly believe fed is best. Period. For me, as a survivor of sexual abuse, connecting to my body in that intentional act of nourishing my child was crucial to my healing. Other survivors find it triggering. You do you, as long as you're feeding yourself and, if you're a parent, your children.)

The pain wasn't over yet. I'd have a dozen more MRSA skin infections. My toddler would have her soothing habit stripped away when the thumb-sucking callous on her thumb became similarly infected. The depletion of all good bacteria in my gut led to some nasty flourishing there of less desirable kinds. My intestines became infected. I lost twenty-one pounds in twelve days. Somehow, through all that, my breasts kept making plenty of milk. Evidently, my body knows how to fall apart in a dozen different ways but it can lactate through malnutrition. That's my superpower.

The infections weren't the only way my body was falling apart. My thyroid disease was under control, but nothing else was. I was in intense pain every day for three years straight, starting before the pregnancy with Robbie and extending a couple of years after. I would wake up first thing in the morning and try to stay perfectly still as long as I could. I didn't hurt yet in the morning. That is, until I moved and my joints told me how much they hated me. So I froze that moment as long as I could before I had to get up.

Most of our friends were in their midtwenties like me. None had walked with someone through the loss, grief, and loneliness of a chronic illness. I could see in some of their eyes that I was their worst fears come true. We were young. We were supposed to be healthy. If my body broke those rules, that meant theirs could too.

We don't like the "I don't knows" of life. We want certainty. We want answers. We're hardwired to figure things out. I get that it was probably scary for our friends to see my health bottom out with no warning. As twentysomethings, few of us had experience with this sort of thing. I imagine they felt helpless and didn't know how to respond. If I could get so sick so fast with no discernible reason for it, so could they. Facing our own mortality and vulnerability isn't a favorite pastime when you're in your twenties, yet I was a walking reminder.

(Now I'm even more so, as the newly widowed single mom of six in my thirties.)

————

The hand that some of us were dealt at a young age has health repercussions today.

Bessel van der Kolk writes in his excellent work *The Body Keeps the Score* about the research linking autoimmune disorders and other health conditions with untreated trauma. It's like in the Bible when the crowd is admonished that the rocks will cry out if the people don't lift their voices in praise for God. Well, if we don't speak the truth about our trauma—not to everyone, of course, but to those who have earned the right to hear it and help us carry it—then our bodies will cry out.

A complicating factor for those of us who have lived through fire is that we don't instinctively know how to live in our bodies anymore. Sure, we survive, but I used to consider my body to simply be the shell I had to wear to carry my mind and soul. This is common:

> Traumatized people chronically feel unsafe inside their bodies: The past is alive in the form of gnawing interior discomfort. Their bodies are constantly bombarded by visceral warning signs, and, in an attempt to control these processes, they often become expert at ignoring their gut

feelings and in numbing awareness of what is played out inside. They learn to hide from their selves.[13]

I didn't realize it, but my body wasn't my home after the years of trauma. I ignored and neglected and wounded it because it felt more like a crime scene than a part of me. Over time, the bottled-up trauma needed to come out, and it didn't always bubble over in pretty ways. I had to learn how to pay attention to my body for another purpose than loathing the skin I was in. My trauma was connected to my body, yes, but my body was also tethered to my trauma. I couldn't ignore one without stunting the other. Again, my experiences are congruent with van der Kolk's work:

> In my practice I begin the process by helping my patients to first notice and then describe the feelings in their bodies— not emotions such as anger or anxiety or fear but the physical sensations beneath the emotions: pressure, heat, muscular tension, tingling, caving in, feeling hollow, and so on. I also work on identifying the sensations associated with relaxation or pleasure. I help them become aware of their breath, their gestures and movements.[14]

We often talk about therapy and other mental health services as if they are meant to treat a psyche independent of the body. That's impossible, though. Whether we acknowledge it or not, we live embodied lives. In one way or another, our body is always keeping score, connected holistically with the rest of our person-hood, just as it was always meant to be.

———

During one of the many health-care debates in recent years, I broke one of my cardinal rules for social media engagement: don't argue with strangers. Period.

Even worse is arguing with strangers on a friend's social media post. Facebook is their online house, and nobody likes when an uninvited rabble-rouser arrives to challenge one of your friends, even if that rabble-rouser is also a friend.

My friend posted about a particularly unjust health-care proposal. Her friend used general terms to say that people need to understand that every medical plan isn't going to work for everyone. I replied with some ways that the specific plan being discussed would be harmful to our family, especially given our chronic health issues and my youngest child's Medicaid pro-gram. I asked, genuinely, if he meant that it was okay with him for us to be affected in this way.

He became upset, even insulting. He said I needed to stop making it personal. This is politics, he said. His words literally took my breath away for a moment. The insides of my nose started to sting, as they always do when I want to cry but haven't given myself permission to do so yet. My chest felt heavy, even pained. Yet I tried to find a way to help him understand. Eventually, the conversation ended with neither of us budging from where we stood as it began.

Politics is always personal. By definition, it's the process and policies impacting us, the people, in our country. We vote because our personal opinions matter. Senators and representatives have staff to answer phone calls from constituents because the personal stories matter. Health-care debates wouldn't be so fraught if they were impersonal. But the health and the care of people is what we're discussing. The people are why politics exist.

I think this gentleman was bothered by my use of story to humanize the issue. It's easy to hold to any position you want if you're considering issues and not people. But when we look each other in the eye, when we listen with our hearts, and when we connect to each other's lived experiences, we change. Our opinions might not, but we show honor to the person in doing so instead of pushing them away as the other. Politics is never about impersonal issues. It's always about people.

We keep our health sacred by connecting to our own personhood. We keep the health of our communities sacred by connecting to the personhood of others. Isolation and independence aren't our best pathways to health. No, we need each other.

———

What's healthy for one person might not be for another. If I'm hurting because of my spinal cord injury, for example, it's healthy for me to take an opioid to control it, as part of the pain management plan designed with my specialist. For others, opioids are addictive and create dependence, proving to be completely unhealthy for them to use.

That's why the health craze online is harmful, driven by diet culture with carefully crafted multilevel marketing companies selling vitality in shakes and supplements. I don't doubt that such paths are healthy for some people, just like milk is a healthy option for me and a terrible choice for my lactose-intolerant best friend. Even the BMI scale has been debunked as a major indicator of health, as we've learned to look at the person and not the numbers, most notably in Health at Every Size (HAES) practices.

Keeping healthy isn't about following other people's rules, because they weren't made for your body. Keeping healthy is about being at home in your body and loving her well. Medical professionals you trust get to weigh in (no pun intended) on what's best for you, and randoms online don't. Yes, I am talking about that friend from high school whom you haven't seen in twenty years but who pops up in your messages to tell you about her new job selling some unproven product because she cares about you, but really she cares about her bank account. Living brave involves saying no thanks or just ghosting her.

PART V

RELATIONSHIPS
ARE BRAVE

CHAPTER 11

HARD CONVERSATIONS

I wish
I could go back
and hold her
protect her
tell her they were wrong
tell her she did nothing wrong
tell her she would one day
live to right all the wrongs
that she couldn't
(and I still can't)
right for her
so I write for her

At the end of our 2019 beach vacation, I had three of the hardest conversations I'll ever have. The final one isn't meant for public sharing because I hold sacred stories like the reactions of my children when I told them Daddy was dead. The first one, though, is when I got the news.

We were in the ICU Family Conference Room. Anyone who

has had a loved one in the ICU knows and hates that room. For the uninitiated, this is the room where they take you to tell you bad news.

I didn't know that. I was expecting to be met at the hospital with the news that Lee was dead, so I felt good knowing he was still alive, even if he was intubated. The doctor's face didn't say much because I'm not sure he has a happy face. If he does, I never saw it.

I couldn't think about this at the time, but this wasn't just a hard conversation for me. This man had worked for hours to stabilize my soul mate, and nothing anyone did would be able to bring him back to us. From Lee's body, the doctor knew he was young and in good shape. With my makeup-free face and ponytail and sand on my legs, I looked younger than my thirty-seven years. This type of news is brutal even when the ages and circumstances make more sense.

As we wrapped up, they brought me to his ICU room. All the wires and tubes and machines were daunting, but I was relieved to see Lee. There he was. He wasn't gone. I could touch him and lay my head on his chest. I put my hand in his, and the doctor immediately noted that Lee was showing more neurological responses to my voice and touch than he had for any of them. I knew from the brain scan that he wouldn't recover, but he was still there, dimly.

Around midnight, the medical team was ready to give him something to help control his blood pressure. They warned me that he would be unresponsive for a bit, so I had a conversation with him—our last—before they put the medicine in his IV. I stood up and held his hand tight and sobbed on his chest, preparing to try to sleep once I left the room. Then we locked eyes, and I whispered firmly, "You have to live, baby. I need you. I need you to stay." He became the most active he had been all night, struggling against his breathing tube as if he was trying to say something, with an intense stare to my soul as if he wanted me to understand something. Seeing him so agitated gave me answers I needed. I brushed my hand across his forehead, pushing his hair to the side, and leaned in.

"Rest, my love." He settled against the pillow, no longer fighting. "You can rest."

Then a mixture of supernatural peace and radical acceptance came over me, as I said, "Just relax. Go to sleep. I'll be okay. You can go and rest." I kissed his cheek.

I knew at my core that these were the last words he would hear before heaven. I watched his eyes close and his body find peace. Then I left to rest myself, knowing I was going to face the unimaginable when I woke up.

And I did.

———

Hope is terrifying. The poet in me feels like I should offer a more flowery appraisal, but the realist in me rejects that idea. I have a T-shirt in my closet with the words "Hope is always worth the risk" in white script on a gray background. Some days

I wear it. Some days I want to burn it. I feel the same about my "This too shall pass" shirt. Occasionally I wear them ironically with my "Nope, not-today" sweatpants.

After contact with my family of origin dried up, I grieved. I still grieve. I watched a door close that I never thought would before my parents and other family members died. Moving on from that isn't possible. It's a pain I carry along with my physical scars at their hands.

It feels foolish to hope, but I still do. I always will. The hope within me doesn't care about reason or logic.

When my sister contacted me in late 2016, I was scared. I wanted to push her away. Lis never hurt me—well, not in any way outside of the typical sister relationship—but we had never been close. I wanted her to be safe, but I feared she wasn't. The most protective act would have been to say thanks but no thanks to her. But a seed of hope in me remained certain that vulnerability was the better path. In this case, vulnerability fit the words said of Aslan by Mr. Beaver in C. S. Lewis's classic *The Lion, the Witch and the Wardrobe*: "Safe? . . . Who said anything about safe? 'Course he isn't safe. But he's good."[15]

"Can we talk?" she asked. I've never been a fan of those three words. They precede hard paths more often than happy ones. But they're also words birthed out of hope. We weren't raised to be hopeful, me and Lis. I knew with those words she was offering the gift of her own vulnerability, with no certainty that I wouldn't stomp on it.

Most of the details that followed are too sacred to share

here, but in early 2017, we were closer than ever. We texted regularly. She and her partner came up to visit near Christmas in 2017, and I planned to head down to Atlanta to see her and get matching tattoos in 2018. I had accepted that I would never have positive family relationships beyond the ones I created with my children, my husband, and his family, but hope told a different story.

Ephesians 3:20 (NIV) comes to mind, describing God as the one "who is able to do immeasurably more than all we ask or imagine." I never could have fathomed this outcome, but my step away from the abuse I endured so long was also a step toward Lis. I have a sister. She is mine, and I am hers. No one can relate to our childhood, not like we can with each other.

The tattoos we planned to get together were the words "I love you," mine in my handwriting and hers in hers, inscribed on our inner wrists. Learning to love ourselves has been a miracle. I didn't used to think it was possible. But here we were, sisters, loving each other and loving ourselves. I'm thankful we both took the risk to talk, making space for this reconciliation.

———

Sadly, reconciliation doesn't always last. I don't know how the story of me and Lis will end, but that last story unraveled, beginning with our dad's death in February 2018. I'm resting in a liminal space in which I hope for restoration in our relationship but have no promise it will come. I posted something on

Twitter, she replied with snark, I texted her with equal snark, and, by the end of the day, she had blocked my number and social media accounts. Then we reconnected when Lee died but only for a month before she got mad at me for not acknowledging her fortieth birthday, which fell three days after the one-month anniversary of Lee's death and two days before what would have been his birthday if he were alive. I could try to explain all of what happened, but that's not a story for public consumption.

It is, however, a story that clearly demonstrates something I've learned from communication studies research, the concept of intent versus impact. Intent is good, but impact is what matters at the end of the day.

Let me unpack that with a simple example. Let's pretend I'm throwing around a Frisbee with a friend when it veers in an unintended direction and strikes a stranger in the face, splitting the skin on his forehead. We apply pressure, wait for an ambulance, and apologize over and over again.

When the Frisbee strikes, the man knows nothing about our intent. (I regularly throw Frisbees off course, so this is not far-fetched.) All he knows is pain and blood in the immediate aftermath. Whether I intended to hit him or not isn't his concern. No, the impact is primary. My intent? Secondary.

Intent matters when it comes to criminal charges because premeditation plays a role. So does malice, but harmful impacts don't require malice. "But I didn't mean to . . ." doesn't change what happened. Maybe it influences how the relationship will continue in the future because something with negative impact is easier to forgive and reconcile if the intent wasn't to be harmful. But intent is about the outcome.

If a reckless driver strikes a pedestrian, harming or killing the person, then the grieving family will still grieve the death of their loved one, whether the driver intended the outcome or not. If food is improperly prepared and then served to people who become dangerously ill, I don't think they care much about intent as they're hugging the toilet. Returning to the original Frisbee example, commonly used in textbooks, saying "I didn't mean to do that" isn't a magic spell that immediately heals the laceration. No, the impact is the outcome, no matter what the intention was.

I don't know what my sister's intent was when she seemed to value her birthday over my grief, but the impact was something neither of us wanted. I hope someday she'll be open to communication again, but as hard as this is to say, it will only work if the hard conversations can continue instead of hardening hearts that replicate abusive systems from our childhood.

———

"Can I come over so we can talk?" Those words came years ago, when Lee was still alive. This is how I measure time now, before and after.

I didn't hesitate to say yes to the question. Liselotte was an adult now, but I met her when she was fourteen. I was a volunteer with the youth ministry at our church, and she was one of my kids.

Liselotte stopped attending church not long after I stopped volunteering with her group. I didn't know this then, but as I continued to serve in various leadership roles at the church, her trust in me dwindled. She knew some secrets I didn't know. She didn't trust the leadership, so she couldn't trust me as a leader. When I finally left, not long before her question, she felt comfortable talking to me about what had been covered up.

I didn't know that when I said we could talk. I didn't know it had anything to do with church. I simply said yes because I've always liked Lise, not because I expected the conversation to be a significant one.

I knew that Doug, a youth ministry intern at our church, had been arrested just a few weeks before I met Lise for the first time, when she was a rising freshman in high school. I hadn't known he was a sexual predator, but he had preyed on several middle school boys in our church. The night he was arrested, the police found him and one of the boys in his car at a park well after dark.

I didn't know that Liselotte had been in Doug's Sunday school class. As she describes it, "I loved that class. It was the first place I felt at home . . . since my family switched to Sunday morning two years prior. Most of the kids in the class were kids I had known at Saturday night church, and the only other girl in the class quickly became the best church friend I had ever had. I thought Doug was hilarious and charming and basically one of the coolest people on the planet." She hadn't known or suspected anything about his crimes either. Even worse, she struggled with feeling like something must have been wrong with her if she connected so well with a pedophile.

The biggest thing that she knew and I didn't, not until that talk between us at my house, was that some of our church leaders were lying when they said there had been no red flags or signs of concern before the arrest. A year before, a boy had come forward with allegations. They were mostly dismissed, with shame heaped upon the boy for his role in what happened. His honesty and mental health were questioned, while questions about his sexuality were raised.

I didn't want to believe her, but Liselotte is a truth teller. She's spoken some truths to me that I'd rather have left unspoken altogether. She might be blunt at times, but she's honest. More than that, she shared documented proof I could review and names of other people involved back then who I could interview. Just like I knew Liselotte to be honest, she knew I needed any confirmation she or others could provide. I am and always have been a research nerd.

Liselotte and I were just beginning to get to know each other all over again at that point. I couldn't have guessed that we'd bring her to our new church, and then when she left there, she'd ultimately bring us to her new church. I didn't know we'd text each other daily. I didn't know we'd grow so close that Lise called me first after her parents when she got engaged. I also didn't know that I—a lover of rest and sleep—would love her enough to FaceTime in the middle of the night to hear the news.

Now, we're better together. We're truly friends turned family. I need her, and she needs me. We could have missed out on all of this if she hadn't taken the risk of asking if we could talk and if I hadn't taken the risk of saying yes.

———

I am certain we need to be having powerful conversations in public spheres, but I chose to focus on interpersonal communication in this chapter. Why? Well, my background is in interpersonal communication studies, but that's not it. No, I'm certain that we can't do right in the larger conversations if we haven't mastered the smaller ones.

That said, sometimes the opportunity arises for entry into a larger conversation. This happened for me in May 2019, as state after state passed draconian laws to limit women's choices when pregnant.

I used to speak at pro-life conferences, and I still hold as dear friends many who are in favor of forcing birth as the only legal option for expectant women. Even by their standards, though, these new laws were dangerously restrictive. No matter the reason, no matter the health of the mother, no matter if the fetus has a condition incompatible with life, these lawmakers didn't differentiate. Continuing pregnancy to natural birth—or fetal or maternal death—was the only option permissible under the laws that swept through the South in the late spring of that year.

With both confidence that the timing was right and heaviness in my chest from the gravity of the decision, I realized I was ready to share my deepest trauma story in the public sphere. I wouldn't advise going from a handful of people knowing your private pain to writing a viral *USA Today* op-ed without any steps in between, but that's what I did. I decided to write the piece Tuesday. I sent it along with a pitch to the editor the same day. It was published the next morning. Less than twenty-four hours passed between my deciding to write and my watching online as friends and strangers and politicians and critics and allies debated my perspective and my personhood, even whether I was real or a "crisis actor." By that night I was on the evening news, then CNN and HLN the next day, and the BBC the following morning.

I don't regret any of it, though the next time I do something like it, I hope my regular therapist will be in town and not on bereavement leave. She returned to the office the following Monday, having been largely unplugged and completely unaware of my media appearances. Surprise!

I was nervous as I read the words to her, the ones published online the previous Wednesday and in the print version of the paper over the weekend. More than anyone else, she knew my path to being emotionally well enough to write such a piece was like rebreaking a poorly set bone so it could heal properly. I had to reckon with ashes and agony and horror before I could rise to write what *USA Today* released into the world. I began the piece by identifying with an eleven-year-old abuse survivor whose story was being used in the debate without her permission.

———

Here's the *USA Today* piece, unedited from its published form:

I was that 11-year-old pregnant by rape in Ohio, except I had just turned 12 and lived in Florida. There will be more children like us, including in Alabama when its near-total abortion ban, which doesn't include exceptions to rape victims, goes into effect.

Police reports tell the little girl's story: 26-year-old rapist, raped multiple times, pregnant but wouldn't be allowed to have an abortion under a new Ohio law going into effect this July.

News commentators tell her story: some as an example, some as a detractor, some with more concern for their political message than her painful realities.

Twitter is debating her story: her age, her worth, her rapist, her pregnancy, her baby, her fetus, her rights, its rights.

She is 11. She has experienced and is experiencing violating trauma. Maybe someday she will tell her story, but today is not that day.

I can tell my story, though. I was newly 12. I lived in a suburb of Tampa. I had gotten my period a couple years before, and it came regularly once it started. I knew to expect it every 32 days.

It was July, the summer between sixth and seventh grade, when days 33, 34, 35 and more passed with no period. I had read in one of my sister's *Seventeen* magazines that periods aren't always regular, so I figured this was my first one of those.

It wasn't.

When I was two weeks late, I threw up for the first time. I was confused initially, because it didn't feel like my experiences with stomach bugs or bulimia.

Then I remembered when Becky from "Full House" had been sick and pregnant with their twins. I did the math. Then I walked a mile-and-a-half to the store, lied to the clerk about needing to get one for my mom, stuck the bag in my fanny pack and began the walk home. Once I got to a familiar grove of trees, I walked in deep, smacking at mosquitoes along the way, until I knew it was safe. I took off my sandals and shorts and underwear, the kid kind with some cartoonish character on them. I read the instructions in detail, three times.

Then I took the test, put on my clothes again and climbed a tree, test in pocket, to wait for the answer. While I waited, I picked at my skinned knee until it started bleeding.

As soon as I saw the results, I scrambled back down the tree to double-check the box. The results were clear. I was six weeks pregnant, and seventh grade was starting at the end of the month.

I've left out a key detail. I never chose to have sex at such a young age, but abusers in my family chose to rape me. I had lost count of the number of times by then. With a dad high ranking in the county sheriff's office, I didn't trust going to the police. I had tried to tell teachers and church volunteers, but that never went anywhere, either.

But I felt like this pregnancy brought hope, so much so that I named the baby inside me Hope. I was sure Hope's existence would bring about change. No one could deny my abuse with genetic proof. I thought my parents would make me quietly get an abortion if I told them, so I didn't. I carried Hope and secrets into seventh grade.

I'm not going to share the sacred details of when my hope and my Hope died a couple months later, as I had a miscarriage before I knew what one was. But I thought about those moments when I read about the 11-year-old girl in Ohio. She can't tell her story, so I'm telling mine.

I need you to know that any child's pregnancy is the result of rape, because no child can consent to sex. I need you to know that any child's pregnancy is traumatic, no matter the outcome, because little girls aren't supposed to have full wombs. I need you to know that I didn't know I had options, because I knew girls who got pregnant were called sluts and girls who had abortions were called murderers.

And I need you to know that if I had lived under the

Ohio law recently passed, I would have been too late to consider abortion by the time I realized I was pregnant. And if I had lived under the Alabama bill likely to be signed into law, being a repeated rape victim wouldn't have given me any options.

If my life were in imminent danger, the Ohio law would permit a later abortion, but being gangly and pregnant at age 12 isn't a life risk.

I know responses to my story will include ones about how what happened to me is rare. I'm the exception, not the norm, they'll say.

But I need you to know that every story is unique. Every discussion of abortion between a woman and her doctor is different. Something that might put one mother's life or health at risk might not be a problem for someone else.

This is why abortion can't be dictated by legislators. This is why abortion decisions must be made individually, between a woman and her doctor.

That Ohio girl's story is being used as a prop in political discourse, but abortion rights matter because she isn't an object. She is a person, same as me when I was 12 and pregnant.

Our humanity matters, in both debates and legislation.

———

I chose to enter this hard conversation about abortions and laws because I didn't see my voice there yet. No one was representing girls like twelve-year-old me as decisions were weighed and de-bated. A nonconsenting eleven-year-old girl was being used like a prop, as if it were okay to share her story for political purposes as long as her name wasn't published. (It was legal to use her story, of course, but what's legal isn't always what's right.)

It would have been acceptable to never tell the story of Hope to anyone other than my closest confidants. That's the thing about public conversations: no one is obligated to have them. We can't wimp out on person-to-person contact, avoiding hard conversations there, but person-to-public disclosures have no rules. Sure, sometimes we say we should write from scars and not wounds, but a few of my most powerful pieces of writing didn't come from a healed place. Will Hope's life and death when I was twelve ever become a scar? I don't know. I'm thirty-seven now, and it certainly isn't showing signs of healing over anytime soon.

One thing I know for sure: surviving is the bravest act, not sharing. I heard from other women in the wake of the media frenzy, and many of their messages began, "I'm not brave enough to share publicly yet . . ." Hear me clearly on this: you never have to enter the public conversation to be brave. For me, that's the right forum for some of my stories. For you, it may never be. My best friend barely uses social media, but she is more bold and honest in personal conversations than anyone I know. Your Twitter feed—or whether or not you use Twitter at all—isn't the metric for your courage. Often it requires more courage to discern what isn't meant for public consumption than it does to click POST or TWEET or PUBLISH.

I still feel nauseated by the vulnerability of telling such a personal story so publicly, but for me—and for this country, I think—it was right and good and maybe even a little redemptive.

Hard conversations usually are.

CHAPTER 12

CHOSEN FAMILY

a fire burns
in her eyes
in her heart
in her soul
in her brain
in her art
in her words
some say
"too much"
and try to pour water
or words over her
to extinguish her flame
others say
"oh, what magnificence"
and offer kindling
and space
and air
to see her whole heart
grow bigger and brighter
—let's all be the latter

miss my husband. He was my deepest and most profound chosen family. We met and chose each other every single day.

He had family before me. I had people who shared my DNA but never acted like family. Those people shared a last name with me for twenty-three years, but they were abusive, even on the day when Lee and I formally chose each other.

I wore a white dress, wondering the whole time if I was worthy of that, having been raped so many times. I didn't know yet, on that day I walked down the aisle to Lee, that nothing about my many sexual assaults made me dirty. Nothing about crimes against my body made my white dress wrong.

I refuse to let that June day in Rio Grande City, Texas, be defined by the inappropriate touches and whispered emotional abuse of my unchosen family. No, it was a day marked by creating our new family, me and Lee.

It was also a day marked by our chosen family. My best friend, Brenda, was my matron of honor; her husband, Rolando, was one of Lee's groomsmen. Other friends who were like family (a group I call "framily") stood with us, and the witnesses to our vows were mostly framily members as well. We chose them and they chose us, mutually out of our reciprocated love and care and acceptance.

For me, chosen family was the only family who offered the love I deserved. I had begun to choose my framily by going to the University of North Carolina at Chapel Hill for college, not knowing a single person there but knowing it was a long drive from my parents' home in Tampa. Then when I moved to Texas,

I gathered more framily. All along, all my life, I was creating a family based in love rather than biology and beatings.

My created family has held me through pain and joined me in celebration and shown up everywhere in between. They remind me to breathe when it's all too much, and they bring pizza when they know dinner—the meal Lee always cooked—feels daunting to me. They send me memes, offer wild ideas like renting out a movie theater for just us in the midst of COVID-19, and arrive at my front door when they know I'm in an unhealthy isolation pattern. They've driven me to therapy, to medical procedures, to the estate attorney's office, to the funeral home, to the cemetery, so I don't have to face them alone. Upon Lee's death, they became the emergency contacts for the kids, the medical decision makers when I'm in surgery, the couples who would raise my six children if anything happens to me.

I am not exaggerating when I say that my chosen family, my framily, has saved my life.

———

Adoption is often linked to the term "chosen family," but I want to be abundantly clear that this is not what I mean.

Adoption is not what I consider chosen family.

If I were tweeting this, some of my words would be in all caps. Yes, I'd be yelling. It matters that much to me.

I am an adoptive mom. I have nothing against adoption, though I believe we should more closely examine the ethics of how it works. Because of stories that led us to give birth to two children and then to adopt one little girl from Taiwan and then to adopt three siblings from Uganda, I'm raising six beautiful children who took different paths to joining the Dingle family. Lee and I made a variety of choices to create our family as it is now.

But if I were to describe us all as chosen family, then I would be centering my experience. Children have no choice in becoming part of their families of origin by birth, and adopted children have even less power over the family decision-making that leads to joining a new family. We chose to adopt the four children who joined our family; they didn't choose us. Even when kids are old enough to be involved in adoption decisions, as is the case in many foster systems once a child reaches a certain age, their possible decisions are limited by the system, and making a choice between option A and option B doesn't mean either was preferred.

I love being the mom of each of my children. I consider it an honor, a particularly sacred one for the four whose first families held hopes and dreams for their flourishing, the fruition of which lies in my hands now. I did choose for them to become ours, mine and Lee's and their first family's, knowing we don't replace anything before us, not cultures or languages or family members.

When we first adopted, I probably would have used "chosen family" language. I've been blogging for more than a decade, so odds are good that something I wrote is floating around the internet with word choices around adoption that I wouldn't use now.

So what changed? I started listening well to adoptees, who have taught me how adopter-centered language is hurtful. Their lives changed, for the better or the worse or, more commonly, for the different. The only person who can affirm the ultimate choice in adoption as helpful or harmful or something else altogether is the adoptee, upon reflection as an adult.

I hope my children will agree with the choices we made. I'll respect wherever they land on this. Until then, chosen family doesn't fit because true chosen family requires reciprocal choosing. Until then, we are legal family, which certainly means a lot. But chosen family isn't chosen unless everyone has a choice.

———

Part of being in a family of your mutual choosing is receiving. I'm sure some people struggle with giving, but that's never fit for me. I like to help. I always kept my CPR and first aid certifications current, until I witnessed my husband receiving CPR; I can't renew that one, not yet. I donate. I have burnt myself out in trying to do good for others, while doing harm to myself in the process. I know how to show up for others.

I wasn't used to receiving. I wasn't used to accepting help. I wasn't used to letting others show up for us.

"I'm fine."

"I've got this."

And so on. I have all the words at the ready to tell people that I'm independent.

But? I'm not. I'm a widow. I'm disabled, and my husband was my caregiver at times. I'm a single mom to six kids. All of my kids have experienced life-altering trauma. Some of my kids live with disabilities or diagnoses like cerebral palsy, autism, ADHD, epilepsy, PTSD, anxiety, HIV, and brain injuries. Sometimes, especially in the first year after Lee died, I needed to ask for help for anything from carpool to laundry, errands to making phone calls. One of my neighbors even cleaned out our trash can when maggots had formed in the bottom of it.

I'm learning to embrace the help that's offered instead of bristling at the idea that help is necessary at all. And somehow, the helpers are still here, ready and eager to hear me say yes to community, to not powering through on my own, to loosening boundaries to let others in instead of trying to be an island standing alone.

———

Boundaries are at the heart of the health or lack thereof of families. Our framily honors boundaries, which isn't a given for biological or legal family. Boundaries are, in the definition of Dr. Brené Brown, simply what's okay and what's not okay. In family systems, the norms of the family often override boundaries unless an intentional re-norming is initiated by someone within the system.

I can't tell you how that works, though. I believe most families can create and honor boundaries. But when boundaries are rejected, like they were in my family, re-norming can't happen. So I honestly don't know what it looks like to rebuild healthy systems into a family not founded on them. (I do know such resources exist, though, and I wish you the best in finding the right one for your needs.)

For me, I didn't know I could have boundaries. I was taught that what was okay and what wasn't okay were determined by others, often abusers, and never by me. What I wanted and what I didn't want were irrelevant to my parents. I had no choices.

Many of my queer friends know their identity clearly, but their parents say it's not okay. The boundary they try to demand is that it's not okay for their child, no matter how young or old, to be queer. How can queer people respond to a boundary that literally tells them that who they are is fundamentally wrong or unacceptable?

I believe restoration can happen. I will hope reconciliation is possible with some of my family members, while I know it isn't for others because having raped me repeatedly is a deal breaker.

Can that pain be redeemed? I don't know. But I will always hope. I will always long for the family that made me to love me like healthy families do. I will always yearn for beauty to rise from ashes.

Is redemption possible at all? Yes, absolutely. That's what

chosen family has been for us. Our framily cares about what's okay and what isn't okay for us, and we care about the same for them. We take the hard steps, sit through the necessary grief, use the power of our words with care, wrestle with hard truths, end the need for secrets, push for hard truths, keep the faith (or not), risk hard trust, honor each other's desires and feelings and health, and have the hard conversations.

In other words, we live brave together.

PART VI

HOPE IS BRAVE

CHAPTER 13

HOPE IS THE BRAVEST THING

hope feels fickle
or
maybe
we are the fickle ones
hope waits on us
to match what we believe
and what we do,
to reach out in the danger
of a world where hope isn't always fulfilled
and grab hold of it anyway
because here's the secret:
caution holds no promises of safety either

was never given a middle name. My siblings liked to joke that middle names cost more and our parents didn't want to pay for me. (That's not true. I checked, several times.)

The truth was my parents didn't like anything between

Shannon and Saunders. I learned to write NMN or NMI on forms: no middle name, no middle initial.

"What should my middle name be?" was a fun game we played at sleepovers. Shannon Anna became the early favorite. (Say it out loud, and you'll understand why.) I liked Alexis for a long time, but my parents said no. Shannon Igans was a later nominee. Then I began dating Lee and Shannon Anna resurged, this time in the form of Shannon Anna Dingle Heimer Schmidt, sung with glee.

Once we were engaged, I was scared about my family's reaction to what I planned to be, Shannon Dingle, no maiden name kept. Being a Saunders had meant pain and brainwashing to hate myself, so I had no desire to continue with that name in any capacity.

As we approached our wedding day, I realized I wanted more than a new last name. I wanted a new middle name as well. On our wedding programs, the front read:

Shannon Saunders

&

Lee Edward Dingle

And the back read:

Shannon Hope Dingle

&

Lee Edward Dingle

That's how my parents found out I wasn't keeping Saunders and how our friends discovered I was choosing my own name. My first name was given by my parents and became my own, my last name was given by my husband and has now become my own, and my middle name was all my own.

As I typed this in my first draft in 2019, my legal name is still Shannon Dingle. It turned out that the Social Security office wouldn't let me add Hope without going through the whole legal process to change my name. I planned to, but I never did. The deed to our home stated my name as Shannon Hope Dingle because I expected that to be my full legal name.

Lee would joke that my Hope was illegitimate. But now, as you read this, my legal name change should have gone through. My hope is legitimate, as I describe in the following essays that make up this final chapter.

And my Hope is also legitimate as you hold these words in your hand. As I wrote this book and survived my first year of being a widow, I decided it was time. I'm Shannon Hope Dingle now, legitimately.

It's time for hope for you too. What hope is inviting you to come and maybe stay a bit, maybe stay forever?

... Because We Don't Know It All

I will always
wonder
who I might have been
if I had been
safe
as a child
(and I'd like to gently tell
well-meaning people
to shove off
when they try to wrap pretty bows
of platitudes and proverbs
around my pain
I did not bleed and break
so I could be
the moral
of your story of the world)

I have a Post-it note on my desk with the words, "I don't have to attend every argument to which I'm invited." Part of that is a reminder to spend my time wisely, but the other part is that I know—as do you, having read this far—that I have changed my views enough times to know the only certainty is that there is no certainty.

We live brave because we know the terrain might change or the path might turn. We know that each of the hard truths and the easy connections and the necessary griefs changes us. I miss Lee, but I also miss the me I was before he died. I've changed enough to hold most things loosely.

Lee and I talked about turning forty-eight when our youngest was eighteen, about traveling then and enjoying each other and maybe going back to school or starting a whole new career. Our plans were like an infinite map, just waiting to be explored. Now, the map is still here, but he isn't.

We knew it was right when we got married. Bringing our first two children into the world was right. Adopting four more kids from two continents was absolutely right. Every step we took along the way? I wouldn't change a thing.

Now as I look toward an uncertain future without Lee, I know I could be wrong. I don't know it all. All I know is how to live brave and how living brave has never failed me yet.

. . . *Because None of Us Is Broken*

I had to be
believed
before I could feel
beloved

What do we mean when we call something broken, like a clock or coffee maker or washing machine? (All of those things have broken recently in our house.) We mean it no longer works as it should. It's functioning—or not functioning—contrary to its design.

Humans, though, are meant to endure, resist, fight, fail, win, and cry. Being human is not being broken, no more than being on the ground means a bird can't fly.

Even what some would call significant brokenness, like PTSD, is normal. We weren't made for trauma, but PTSD is something that develops by design when humans experience more than we ever should. I'm calling forth the words of Bessel van der Kolk again because he is both a trauma expert and a skilled communicator:

Long after a traumatic experience is over, it may be reactivated at the slightest hint of danger and mobilize disturbed brain circuits and secrete massive amounts of stress hormones. This precipitates unpleasant emotions, intense physical sensations, and impulsive and aggressive actions. These posttraumatic reactions feel incomprehensible and overwhelming. Feeling out of control, survivors of trauma often begin to fear that they are damaged to the core and beyond redemption.[16]

But are survivors damaged to their core? No. Everything we call brokenness is a human response to a world in which both babies can be born and daddies can die at the beach. We are human. We are not broken, none of us.

. . . Because We All Belong

he didn't heal me
but
his love taught me
I was worthy of healing

I belonged with Lee. We fit together. A part of me still belongs to him and always will.

But I know I can belong elsewhere too. We all belong somewhere.

Whenever I heard anyone mention Martha's Vineyard, Massachusetts, I used to think about fancy vacations for people a few classes above my family. I wasn't even sure it was real. It could have been a fictional vacation spot made up for TV.

Ever since I learned about the history of deafness there, my first thought about that area of the country has centered on when disability isn't disabling. In 1854 in the US, 1 in 5,728 people were Deaf. Meanwhile, the incidence was 1 in 155 on Martha's Vineyard. In the town of Chilmark, it was 1 in 25, rising to 1 in 4 in one part of town.

The Americans with Disabilities Act didn't exist then. Neither did IDEA (Individuals with Disabilities Education Act), the law ensuring a free and appropriate public education to children of all disabilities. No one said, "You must include everyone, hearing or not." No, they knew each other, so they all learned Martha's

Vineyard Sign Language, created on the island for communication on the island. They belonged to each other.

Because deafness was seen as a normal part of their community, Deaf people were involved in every aspect of life there. They could work the same jobs, attend the same events, and eat at the same restaurants as their hearing friends and family. Children, both hearing and Deaf, learned the local sign language from a young age. There was no us and them. They were simply one community.

We haven't seen this outside of small communities, though, maybe because larger communities have strangers while close-knit towns don't. Life with other people is messy, but sometimes we honor one another, like the people on Martha's Vineyard did long ago. Someday, maybe, we can do more of that.

For me, McAlister's Deli in Durham, North Carolina, is a lot like what I think Martha's Vineyard was back then. It's close to my therapist's office, and it feels safe. The staff is mostly people of color, which is also comforting to me. There's one table in particular where the sun hits just right, the power outlet is near enough for plugging in my computer, and I can get both a bowl of chicken tortilla soup and a decadent baked potato with cheese and bacon.

Extra bacon, to be clear.

But it's the personal touch of the staff that's my favorite. They know about my piercings and tattoos; I know about their lives away from the restaurant. We both know which songs make us join along, even though they're supposed to be background music. Just now, one of them brought my order to the table as I was typing out another chapter, and he immediately asked, "Oh, wait, do you want extra tortilla chips?" Of course I did. I always do. He knew that. Being known? That's a precursor to belonging anywhere.

Meanwhile, there's another café I frequent after therapy, a German bakery and restaurant called Guglhupf. By objective standards, the atmosphere is more elegant, the food more highbrow, and the lattes like magic in a mug. I like it there. I've written there. It just looks like a place meant for the author of the next great American novel to do their word-crafting. But by my own subjective standards, it's merely a place where I write sometimes. It's not like home. McAlister's totally is. I belong there in a way I don't at Guglhupf (though "Guglhupf" is decidedly more fun to say).

Often when we're talking about belonging, we think about the basics of group dynamics, or we dive into the deeper waters of feelings. But belonging can be as simple as feeling comfortable in your skin wherever you are. I feel that way at Target and Walmart but not Tuesday Morning or Kmart. I feel that way at our kids' current dance studio, but I didn't at the first studio we tried. I feel that way at any Starbucks because I can predict what it'll be like before I even walk in the door. And that's how I feel about McAlister's.

(I promise, y'all, I do eat and shop local too. But for me, maybe as a facet of PTSD, I feel the most belonging and safety in familiar places. If I'm already in a secure place emotion-ally, new places aren't daunting. Otherwise, I want to know the lay of the land and preferably my intended order before even entering the space. Hate on big chains all you want, but for me—especially when I travel—when I see their signs at the entrance of a strip mall, I feel like I'm Linus finding his trusty blue blankie.)

Sometimes a sense of belonging—in a place, with a person or group, to ourselves—is that Spidey-sense of feeling like it's just right. I call this the Goldilocks test. Is it too hot, too cold, or just right? Is it too firm, too soft, or just right? The converse of this is the Princess and the Pea test. Does something feel wrong, no matter how small it is and no matter if I can't even identify it?

I'm not suggesting we bail every time we don't feel like we belong. A lot of us would be hermits if that were our practice. Doing an internal check of what we're feeling and how our belong-o-meter is working can help us gauge how vulnerable we choose to be or watch for the unspoken rules so we can find more comfort there in our own skin.

Give yourself permission to trust your gut, because until you know and belong to yourself, you can't be known and belong with others.

... *Because the Light Still Shines*

it is human
to age
to breathe
to laugh
to weep
to break
to heal
to love
to need
to be
to do
to rest
to wonder
to create
to live into all you were meant to become
give yourself permission,
love,
to live this gloriously human life
you have been given
it is yours

The day after Lee died, I stepped outside and immediately said, "Well, fuck the sun for shining today like nothing has even changed." I was saying it to Lisa, whose preschool son died four years earlier, so she didn't even flinch. She joined in as I declared the sun to be insensitive and rude.

But it's true: the sun still shines, even when rainy days feel far more appropriate.

The sun was shining at the funeral home, as my two-year-old niece and nephew, Lee's sister's twins, ran all around, beautifully oblivious to our grief and eliciting smiles we didn't think we had.

The sun was shining the day after Lee died, when one of my youngest ones asked my friend Rachel, who had slept on the couch, "So with Dad dead, does that mean we still need to follow his rules?"

The sun was shining when one of my teenagers said, "Hey, Mom, I know everything is hard, but I really like the ways you've been doing things."

The sun has been shining in the way people in our community keep showing up for us in both tangible and intangible ways.

I know how brightly the sun shone on the day of our wedding and at our reception, a carnival we created called Dinglefest, with a bouncy house, a jousting ring, a bungee run, a rock-climbing wall, an obstacle course, Dippin' Dots, pool tables and air hockey tables and foosball tables, video game consoles, and a dunk tank where Lee and I ended up together by the end of it all. I know how brightly Lee would shine as he untaught me all the bad things I believed about myself, lies I had been brainwashed to believe as a child. I know how richly everything shone in Ireland, when we took our first and only child-free vacation together four months before he died.

Because I know the feel of the sun on my skin, I can trust that I will feel it again in the moments where darkness seems like all there is. Holding close the hope that the light will shine again soon when the world is full of shadows?

That's the epitome of living brave.

BENEDICTION

All my love to you,
fellow living braver.
We can dwell in darkness,
looking for the light we once knew,
holding hope that it might shine again,
and doing the next thing until it does.

Shannon Hope Dingle

ACKNOWLEDGMENTS

This book isn't just my labor. It was written in the first year after Lee died, a year in which every breath required the lifting of an impossible weight on my chest. That year included the first five months of COVID-19 and extreme isolation for the health and safety of our family. The words found on each page couldn't have been arranged into anything coherent without a rich community around us, loving us all well in the after and the uncertain. I know how rare and precious that sort of love is. I wish that you, my reader, find the same love in each of your after storms.

I am especially grateful:

. . . for all of you, who knew us and who didn't, who gave to us as the news broke around the world, who lit candles and said prayers and sent notes and meant to send notes but couldn't find the words.

. . . for the journalists who treated our family and story with love and care, especially Diane Wilson at ABC11, Rachel Paula Abrahamson at TODAY.com, and Yonat Shimron and Bob Smietana at RNS.

. . . for my editor, Katy Hamilton, and my agent, Amy Bishop, for believing in my work and coming to me with permission to grieve rather than meet deadlines as soon as Lee died.

. . . to the teams at HarperOne and Dystel, Goderich & Bourret, for all I know that you've done and for all the things I'll never know that you've done for me and this book.

. . . for Lindsey, for immediately coming to the hospital at the beach and caring for me there and coordinating care for months after.

. . . for Rachel. Words fail me right now, but you never have. Glad I can keep your life interesting.

. . . for Angie, your loyalty has taught me how to love and be loved. I'm sorry for all the bad movies.

. . . for Heidi, who saw the brave in me before I knew it was there, and who taught me my trauma doesn't define me. Thank you for bringing your candle into my darkness.

. . . for Laura, who named me a miracle before I knew that word was true.

. . . for Dana, for helping me guide my kids through all this, and for replying to dozens of "Am I a bad mom?" texts.

. . . for Matt, for being present for Lee in life-changing ways and teaching him about empathy. Your wife can rest assured that the dog is safe here with us and was spared Lee's long walk into the woods.

. . . for Frauke, who cares deeply about my work and my rest, and the balance between the two.

. . . for Kathryn, who decoded the email I sent that night,

before I could write the word dead. I am grateful for our friendship and for the ways you've gently punctuated the education of each of my babies (and of me too).

. . . for Mom and Dad Dingle, and for Laurie and Jay, who have been deeply kind and patient as we figure out how to do this whole in-law family thing without Lee. I love you so very much. And thank you for raising the man who loved me and I loved in return.

. . . for Pastor Lisa, for your friendship and for helping me trust the church again.

. . . for Colin, Sarah, and Ada, for becoming family to us.

. . . for Donna, who reminded me again and again "you are loved" in the early days after Lee died and in every day since

. . . for Beth, David, Jessica, David, Kada, Adwoa, A.J., Willie, Phyllis, Burgetta, Nicole, Jordie, Mark, Todd, Caroline, Katie, Alexan, Becky, Kellay, Ken, Frank, Heidi, Kurt, Karmia, Lizzie, Josh, Mary Kate, Kirsten, Emma, Greear, Anna, Rodney, Emory, Chris, Carolyn, Diane, Vaughn, Mark, Tricia, Sarah, Heather, Deidre, Brad, and the rest of my SERT family. You picked me up when I felt beaten by the side of the road, and you retaught me who I was when I forgot, and you showed up again and again.

. . . for Tori and Matt, for coming to our rescue more times than I can count.

. . . for Wonder Woman, for laughing at me as I drink in the rain. (And being helpful and kind, but especially the laughing in the rain.)

. . . for Lise, for believing the best of me, even when I didn't have all the facts to live up to that. Also, for keeping the receipts that prove how deeply evangelical and Republican I once was, and for keeping them private.

. . . for April, Arinn, Christina, Mary, and others who showed up in the first weeks and so many weeks after. I don't even know all of the people who were here, to be honest. I do know that I needed you, and you came.

. . . for all the surgeons, doctors, physical therapists, pain specialists, infectious disease team members, nurses, aides, occupational therapists, speech therapists, and psychiatrists involved in the care and keeping of our family.

. . . for Disabled Twitter, because ableism would suck more without someone to share it with . . . or, um, something like that.

. . . for Andrea, Stephanie, Stephanie, Lindsay, and Kaitlyn, you are the loyal friends I didn't know I needed.

. . . for Andrea and Patti, for your love, and for driving all day to get to me from Canada as soon as I texted that Lee was dying.

. . . for Hannah, for childlike trust and friendship blossoming into grown-up shenanigans, from 1985 to today.

. . . for shorty Ruthie, you showed up to get me to and through the start of school for my babies, the filling out of forms with one parent when there used to be two. And for Louie pics.

. . . for tall Ruthie, if you weren't a part of us, I think we'd all be unhealthy and unhappy, me most of all. We're keeping you.

. . . for big Zoe, who went along for a beach vacation with us in July 2019, just after graduating from college, and didn't know that she would witness Lee's jolting death and then care for our six scared kids while I was at the hospital to be with him as he died. You're amazing, my girl. I'm so proud of all you are and all you're becoming.

. . . for Abby, for pouring yourself into us. You are family, and we are always patagucci grateful for that.

. . . for Lisa, it's totally weird that Eli and Lee share the same deathaversary. Thanks for teaching me to grieve well, because dammit four-year-old boys shouldn't die, and for making me do the necessary things between his death and funeral.

And above everyone else, this is:

for Jocie,

for Patience,

for Philip,

for Robbie,

for Patricia,

for Zoe.

I love being your mama. I like being with you for all the things. It is my greatest privilege to watch you grow up, becoming all you're created to be, even the times when you ask "Wait, this is still the first book, Mama?" or "Why does publishing a book take so long?" or "Focus, Mama!"

Look, my darlings—it's done! I've finally birthed this book baby.

Now let's go get brave milkshakes!

NOTES

1. Donald Hall, "Distressed Haiku," *The Atlantic* 285, no. 4 (April 2000): 98.

2. Jan Richardson, *The Cure for Sorrow* (Orlando, FL: Wanton Gospeller Press, 2016), location 275, Kindle.

3. Brené Brown, "The Power of Vulnerability," filmed June 2010 at TEDxHouston, Houston, TX, video, 20:04, https://www.ted.com /talks/brene_brown_the_power_of_vulnerability?language=en.

4. Bessel van der Kolk, *The Body Keeps the Score* (New York: Penguin, 2015), 235.

5. J. K. Rowling, *Harry Potter and the Order of the Phoenix*, 1st ed. (New York: Scholastic Press, 2003), 824.

6. Coleman Barks, *Rumi: The Big Red Book: The Great Masterpiece Celebrating Mystical Love and Friendship* (New York: HarperCollins, 2010), location 844, Kindle.

7. Archibald MacLeish, *J.B.: A Play in Verse* (New York: Samuel French, Inc., 1958), 18.

8. Diane Langberg (@DianeLangberg), "Abusers often hide behind good deeds, kind words & a good reputation in public," Twitter,

July 11, 2016, https://twitter.com/DianeLangberg/status/
1104079429029036033.

9. Brené Brown, *The Gifts of Imperfection* (Center City, MN: Hazelden, 2010), xii.

10. Frederick William Danker, ed., *A Greek-English Lexicon of the New Testament and Other Early Christian Literature*, 3rd ed. (Chicago: The University of Chicago Press, 2000), 932; New English Translation Bible, note on Philippians 3:8, accessed November 24, 2020, http://classic.net.bible.org/bible.php?book=Phi&chapter=3#n10.

11. Edward Pocock, *A Commentary on the Prophecy of Malachi* (Oxford: Printed at the Theater, 1677; Ann Arbor: Text Creation Partnership, 2011), ch. 2, 19–21, http://name.umdl.umich.edu/A55226.0001.001.

12. J. K. Rowling, *Harry Potter and the Order of the Phoenix*, 1st ed. (New York: Scholastic Press, 2003), 824.

13. Van der Kolk, *The Body Keeps the Score*, 98–99.

14. Van der Kolk, *The Body Keeps the Score*, 103.

15. C. S. Lewis, *The Lion, the Witch and the Wardrobe* (New York: HarperCollins, 1994), 80.

16. Van der Kolk, *The Body Keeps the Score*, 2.